Fighting Back

GEORGINA COLTHURST

Fighting Back

Foreword by HRH The Princess Royal

Methuen London

First published in Great Britain in 1990
by Methuen London, Michelin House, 81 Fulham Road, London SW3 6RB

A CIP catalogue record for this book
is available from the British Library
ISBN 0 413 61460 3

Printed in Great Britain
by Clays Ltd, St Ives PLC

To all those horses
without whose support
I would never have managed
to fight back

List of Illustrations

Acknowledgements and thanks for permission to reproduce photographs are due to Tom Hustler for plates 1b and 15b; Wallace Heaton for plate 2b; John Hinde for plate 3a; Photonews for plates 4a and 5b; Monty for plate 5a; Clive Hiles for plates 6a and 13b; John Taylor for plate 6b; *Eventer* for plates 7a, 13a and 14a; Photo Delcourt for plates 8a and 8b; Barn Owl Associates for plate 14b and Paul Green for plate 16.

Georgina Colthurst was a normal, happy teenager who was shortlisted for the Junior European Three-Day Event Championships when disaster struck.

This story of Georgina's remarkable comeback from a horrendous riding accident which left her unconscious for seven weeks (with only a fifty-fifty chance of survival) with a severe head injury and paralysis down one side from which few felt she would ever recover is told twelve years later.

It recounts all the frustrations and anguish she felt but was unable to communicate at the time because of her severe speech problems and confused brain patterns and the struggle to relearn everything once again from all the basic functions and how to eat, dress, communicate as well as talk and walk.

Georgina's determination to ride again despite her injuries became her driving force.

Georgina's recovery and overcoming her problems of concentration, balance, speech and coordination and the specialist help she received from so many to achieve this resulted in her passing Pony Club A test and The British Horse Society's Intermediate teaching exam. She also came back to compete in Advanced Horse Trials and was selected to ride for Britain at the Boekelo Three-Day Event in Holland.

The book has been written in the hope that it will help others who have suffered similar injuries to keep fighting back. 'When you've got to face something – you have no option.' What an example Georgina has set.

Anne

Nothing benefits more the inside
of a man than being outside on a horse

Sir Winston Churchill

Prologue

I had doubts about writing this book, but I was persuaded by friends that it might be helpful to injured people and their relatives. I would far rather have tried to jump the big wall at the Horse of the Year show, but for a number of reasons I have decided to take the bit between my teeth.

I had a riding accident when I was sixteen, and nearly died. In fact, some people gave me up for dead and very few thought that I would make an almost complete recovery. During my rehabilitation, I have come across many people who have suffered from similar injuries who, despite the loving help from family and friends, doctors and nurses, church people and therapists, have failed to recover – perhaps because they did not believe in the possibility.

My personal experience has been with head injuries, and of course some injuries are far worse than others, but my observation of many people who have been similarly injured, coupled with my own experiences, has taught me that a combination of the right care and a positive attitude on the part of the injured person can lead to unexpected recovery.

Many injured people despair. That is quite understandable. When stories of my own personal accident and recovery began to circulate, I was surprised to receive letters from all over the world, mostly from the families of injured people, asking me how I had overcome my problems and what advice I could offer them.

That was the impetus for this book. I decided that if my experience could help others, I ought to record it, and I was encouraged to do this by a number of people, including Rosemary Manning, a friend who introduced me to literary agent Jeffrey Simmons, without whom this book would never have been written. I am deeply grateful to him. Nearly forty people were interviewed for the book, notably those who could fill the gap in my life when for seven weeks I was unconscious. Some of their testimony is recorded here; I am greatly indebted to these busy people, and of course to my family, who found time to talk about me for the purpose of this book. Thanks to Frank Andrews, Corinne Barnett, Janet Biddle, Teresa Elwell, Major Charles Jones, Harold Judd, Haakon Lovell, Pat Manning FBHS, Rosemary Manning, Jacky Martin-Betts, Tessa Martin-Bird FBHS, Caroline Mooring, Deliah Moseley, Glenn Neil-Dwyer FRCS, George Northcroft FRCS, Maggie Nicholls, Lady Raeburn, Deirdre Robinson, 'Nan' Scott, John Smart, Charles Stratton, Nigel Taylor, Solihin Thom, Jacqueline Tennant, Colin Wares, Anthony Webber, Diane Wilson.

Recalling everything, over twelve years after my accident, has not been easy, and these people have helped me to understand how, from paralysed coma and the brink of death, I managed to fight my way back to something like my normal self. It is embarrassing to read what they have said about my courage and determination. Only I know the anguish and frustration I went through, but when you have got to face something, you have no option.

If my story can help even one injured person to make the best of his or her disability and recover, I shall be glad I have told it.

The Accident

The accident happened on Friday, 3 June 1977. I was due to sit my 'O' levels later that day in Biology and English Literature, but I always rode before school and today was no different. I wanted to practise Tantivy over some fences because he had had a slight problem at a show the previous weekend, so I hacked him about a mile to the equestrian centre at Coakham, which we reached at about 7.30 am.

Tantivy, reputed to be a half-brother of Marion Mould's famous show-jumping pony, Stroller, was a small bay horse, aged nine at the time. He was just over pony height. He was the only horse we then had at home. There were also two ponies, Snoopy and Tiny. Tantivy had been with the family a couple of years. What he lacked in beauty, he made up in character. I had taught him to shake hands and he had a naughty habit of trying to climb trees with his back legs. He was asthmatic and had trouble at times with his breathing, but this only worried him in tremendous heat. Although 3 June was a dry, hot day, he did not seem much affected in the early morning. What I loved about him was that he seemed to have a fifth leg – he was extremely clever on his feet.

I was planning to ride him for up to half an hour and then hack back to change for school, where I was due at 8.45. At the weekend show he had been landing rather short over the fences and finding it difficult therefore to achieve the right distances between doubles and trebles, so I planned that morning to help him lengthen his stride between fences. We had done this sort of gridwork together many times before.

But we were not to do it again, and I was not to do

anything else for a long time. We approached the first grid; without rising an inch Tantivy caught the pole between his legs, dropped his shoulder and we crashed down . . . I seem also to remember being lifted off the ground into darkness, but I cannot be sure of anything else that happened over the next few weeks except a jumble of sensations: dark shapes, ballooning heads, grey smudges of faces, murmuring voices, sliding in and out; dryness, like a thick duster in my mouth; a huge thirst; cold as well; the smell of a damp cloth and scented soap; all woolly and dim . . .

Background

I am my parents' only daughter. I have three older brothers. I was born in London on 16 February 1961, and was brought up mainly in Kent in the family house where my parents have lived for over thirty years. Most of our holidays were spent in Ireland with my maternal grandparents or at my father's farm in County Cork. This is quite a notable place because it includes the famous Blarney Castle in its grounds, and my father owns the Blarney Stone, which has been in the family for many generations.

People who once kiss the Blarney Stone are reputed to be blessed with the gift of eloquence. The stone is underneath the castle battlements and you have to lean over backwards to kiss it, so it is not all that easy, but I have kissed it many times and perhaps that will help me to tell my own story!

It was in Ireland that I first sat on a horse. I was not yet three years old when I asked to sit on my mother's hunter, Linnet, and almost immediately my grandfather bought our first pony, Dolly, for my brothers and me. We all rode in turns. I loved Ireland and the Irish people, and have always looked forward to the times I spent there. My father's family, originally from Yorkshire, went to Ireland in 1589. The baronetcy started in 1744 and my father is the ninth holder.

He has been at Lloyd's for most of his working life and my eldest brother, Charles, who is trained in the law, runs the family estate in Ireland. His is a full-time occupation because visitors come from all over the world to see Blarney Castle, its gardens and The Rock Close, containing supposedly Druidic stones and wishing steps. It is a romantic place.

My mother, born Janet Wilson-Wright, comes from a distinguished Irish family. Her grandfather was Sir Almroth Wright, who developed the anti-typhoid vaccination and founded the Wright-Fleming Institute at St Mary's Hospital, Paddington, where Sir Alexander Fleming discovered penicillin. James, my second brother, is a medical man. He is a qualified surgeon but is currently involved in hospital administration and management. My youngest brother, Henry, has followed my father into the City, specialising in bloodstock insurance.

I started riding in our local village when I was aged four, with a wonderful lady called Miss Rogers. One of the things I remember most was her insistence on all the bits being thoroughly washed after every ride. I later fell in love with a pony called Tiny at my local riding school and was overjoyed when my parents bought him for me. I rode him every day when I could after school and at weekends. We had no stable for him at home at the time and he was entrusted to Janet Suckling, my riding teacher.

Tiny was a very naughty pony originally, but we soon got

used to each other. He became expert at dressage and by the time I was eight we were a very successful pair. He died three years ago.

My next ponies were Zahra and Spring, who gave me experience in the show ring. Snoopy started me off jumping competitively. Part of the fun was travelling and coping generally, and I think that was when I began to formulate the sense of routine, organisation and discipline that stood me in good stead on the way back from my accident.

Two years later Janet Suckling gave up her stable and suggested that I approach Deirdre Robinson, who lived only nine miles away. She was regarded as an excellent horse trainer and riding teacher, and we soon formed a great friendship. Among other things, she taught me to ride sidesaddle and persuaded Mum that it would be a good idea to buy Witch, who came to us as an unbroken three-year-old and who was to carry me faithfully at sidesaddle competitions, culminating in our coming second at the Royal International Horse Show at Wembley in 1974.

Within my first year with Deirdre I was winning classes on her ponies also. One great day came when I displayed Oberon, her super dressage horse, at Olympia each day. I was eleven years old at the time.

It was in 1972 that we came by Tantivy, who four years later fell, and so occasioned this book. He was not the 'wonder pony' we had been looking for and it was a year later that we found *her*. Tom Parker, the ex-show-jumper, had been looking out for suitable ponies for us and asked us to go to Worcester Park to see a highly recommended bay. As soon as I set eyes on her, fourteen hands high, I thought our journey had been wasted. She had been ill and looked very sluggish. I rode her and at first despaired at her lack of spirit, but we bought her nevertheless. At home she slowly recovered and the very first time I took her across country in a Pony Club team event, I felt a new thrill.

We named her Minnehaha, and of course she was known as Minnie. She was just tremendous. She moved like silk, sped like a bullet, jumped everything as though it were not there. She went on to take me to France in 1974 in a British pony team, and we came second, only one point behind the winning Swede.

Of all my riding activities – showing, Pony Clubbing, eventing, dressage and hunting – eventing was what I liked best, perhaps because it combines them all. My first big prize was on Tiny, for dressage, in 1969. My greatest thrill, however, came when I was eleven, when I won my first Pony Club event.

Of course I was lucky to have parents who could afford to indulge my interests and who enjoyed helping me, and I often wonder what, if anything, I would ever have achieved in this field without them.

I became bitten by the eventing bug when, in 1973, at the age of twelve, I was picked for my Pony Club Horse Trials team. I should perhaps explain what eventing is. In its most basic form it consists of three disciplines – dressage, show-jumping and cross-country.

Dressage is an obedience test for a horse in which it is required to perform selected movements in harmony with the rider, rather similar to skating figures on ice. Unlike show-jumping and cross-country, it does not involve leaving the ground. Show-jumping of course takes place in an arena over collapsible fences whereas cross-country demands jumping a large variety of fixed obstacles.

I had had some experience of all three elements at different times but I had never had to do all three in one day with the same animal, which is the whole point of eventing. Some horses are better at one discipline than at others, as indeed are some riders, and a good partnership in which horse and rider can help each other is most important.

I was riding Tantivy that year. His strength was show-jumping. He did not mind any cross-country fences but his mischievous nature sometimes got the better of him, particularly in woodland where he seemed sometimes more interested in admiring the scenery than in getting on with the job. He thought dressage a boring waste of time and would grind his teeth. A favourite trick was to kick at the judges' cars, which is hardly a requirement!

Next year Minnie took his place and made my life a lot easier because she was much better than him at dressage, equally good at show-jumping, and at cross-country she was quite incredible. She was a bad starter, but once over the first two fences, she was brilliant, neat as a cat. I remember the Pony Club Championships at Stoneleigh that year when a lot of competitors were having trouble at one particular big fence – a very dark sleeper table, recently creosoted and shining dazzlingly in the sun. She approached it a little too fast and most of the spectators, I later learnt, thought that she would join the other horses who had stopped or fallen. But somehow she rose like a helicopter and cleared it easily. We finished eighth overall. I was the youngest competitor out of fifty.

The excitement of being selected for an official British

team is something I can never forget. I owe a lot to Folly, my first real horse, who also came to me via Tom Parker. The first time I took him across country, a new experience for him, he fell and I broke my collarbone. I had fallen many times but this was the first occasion on which I had done any damage to myself, and I was out of action for three weeks. But Folly made up for his mistake – or probably mine! – a thousandfold. He became so good and successful that we were selected for the Junior European.

I was at home one evening in late April 1977 when the telephone rang. I answered it, and it was Colonel Allfrey for me. He was Chairman of the Junior Selectors and he asked me to take part in the final selection trial at the Tidworth Three-Day Event in May. I was quite amazed, having had no warning or expectation of such a possibility. I thanked him and rushed in to tell my parents.

Tidworth was in fact my first three-day event and Folly did me proud. We were fourth in the dressage, our most difficult test to date, and went through the other phases without penalty, so finishing fourth overall. I was told afterwards that I was on the shortlist for Fontainebleau, and it was generally assumed that I was on the team. The eight people on the shortlist had to be available for training.

I now set my sights on Fontainebleau in August. Also on the shortlist were Suzanne May, daughter of Peter May, the English cricketer, and my friend Belinda Davies. This was a heady time for me and it was difficult to concentrate on schoolwork.

Unfortunately, Fontainebleau was not to be – at least not for me – not because I was not selected, but for the totally unforeseen reason that I had the accident which was to change my whole life and from which at one time it looked as though I would never recover.

I seem somehow vaguely to remember being taken to the Kent and Sussex Hospital but it may be that I am imagining this in the light of what I later learnt. I was taken to the Casualty department of that hospital immediately, but I cannot be certain of anything before I regained consciousness in St Thomas's Hospital. I am told that I was completely paralysed for two and a half weeks, and I was still paralysed on my left side when I regained consciousness. I was terrified: I could not move, talk or communicate in any way. I thought I was having a bad dream, but it did not go away. People I recognised began to drift into my vision, especially my family, and I could hear them talking without being able to recognise what they were saying. I wondered why I could see Big Ben through a window and I thought I was not myself. The real me should have been riding and completely independent. I did not have a proper grip on reality. It was only later that I knew that seven weeks had passed between my accident and my first awareness of my new situation.

Lady Colthurst (mother)

I suppose most of our generation remember 1977 as being Jubilee year, the Queen's twenty-fifth year on the throne. It was also the year Virginia Wade won Wimbledon.

Certainly the celebrations round and about in Kent and London had started early that hot summer.

Most of the towns and villages were decorated with flags, bunting and flowers, and the countryside looked extremely festive. Added to which, it was one of the finest years for roses, and every garden was ablaze with their blooms.

I remember that it was a perfect English summer morning with a balmy breeze blowing in from the Vale of Kent below us. In hot weather we are lucky the house is so high on the hills as there always seems to be plenty of air.

Richard, my husband, had his usual summer swim before breakfast, which we always had early so that Georgina could ride before school. In the summer it is so much pleasanter to do most of our daily chores and exercise before the sun is fully out.

Georgina got Tantivy tacked up, and I heard her trotting down the road. She was anxious to give him a quick practice over fences before school, but it was important that she should not be too long as she had her second lot of 'O' levels that day at St Michael's – about three miles away. She had been studying until late the night before for English Literature and Biology, and the exams certainly would not wait for her.

Richard dashed off to collect a load of shavings before going up to the City and I was alone in the house twenty minutes later when the phone rang. It was the Coakham head groom to say they had found Georgina unconscious after a fall, and she had just been taken by ambulance to the Kent and Sussex Hospital in Tunbridge Wells, fifteen miles away.

They said they had seen Georgina arrive and go to the jumping paddock, and the next thing Tantivy had come back to the stables with no rider, so they had rushed down and found her on the ground. The ambulance had come immediately. I asked how badly she was hurt but they were unable to tell me.

I must have felt as shattered as any other mother when I put down the telephone. It all seemed unreal. Cakes in the oven were forgotten as I rushed to the car, and to my relief met Richard coming in the gate, so we were able to leave together.

Georgina was in Casualty but we were not allowed to see her properly, only to peep through a glass window in the door. She seemed to be lying on a white bed – still in her jodphurs and shirt. Her face was chalk white and her right arm and leg were jerking convulsively.

A grave-faced Dr Morris led us into the corridor.

'I'm afraid it's extremely serious,' he said, 'but more than that I can't tell you, because it's a head injury and we can't diagnose or treat that properly here. I don't know what occurred. The horse apparently went back to the Coakham stables. The grooms had seen Georgina earlier, so they knew where she was going. Then they found her lying on the ground, under the trees. The ambulance went immediately.'

Richard asked what her prospects were.

'Head injuries are hardest of all,' said the doctor. 'But I'm afraid you should prepare yourselves. I put her chances of recovery at only fifty-fifty. I have to warn you she may be dying.'

Through a numbness I could feel the doctor's compassion as Richard asked what was the next thing to do.

'She has to have specialist neurological treatment immediately,' said the doctor. 'And we can't do that here. The Brook Hospital up at Blackheath is the nearest facility. We're checking now to see if they can take her.'

There was nothing we could do to help and we felt quite useless for what seemed a very long time until at last we were back in the car. The next two hours were the longest I can remember, until suddenly we were hurrying towards London, trying to keep up with the ambulance in the thick summer traffic. Somewhere – I think in Catford – we lost them, and we had to keep stopping to ask the way to Shooter's Hill.

We first saw the Brook as a sprawling Victorian red-brick edifice on the open slopes before Blackheath, next to the imposing frontage of the derelict Royal Herbert Hospital. Both had been built, with wards designed by Florence Nightingale, principally for fever patients from our then far-flung Empire.

The Brook contained, for the South East region, a complete neurosurgical unit fully equipped with a scanner and all other modern technology. The unit consisted of two large wards, one for men, one for women. There were people of all ages suffering from strokes, brain tumours, meningitis and the like.

These huge wards ensured isolation for each bed, so maximising the air flow while minimising risk of infection. The patients had enough privacy, but could still communicate with their next-door neighbours if they wanted to. The wards were always bright and airy, and infinitely preferable to many of the modern ones with plate-glass windows and air conditioning.

Under the white coverlet Georgina seemed quite still at first. There was a tube running into her nose, but what really shocked us was that the whole of the left side of her head had been shaved, down to the skull – the dark brown hair had vanished. Her eyes were closed in a dreadfully pallid face, with a mottled bruise on her left cheek. We waited patiently, listening and watching for any little sound or movement.

Richard had telephoned the boys, and first James arrived from St Thomas's Hospital. Then Charles came hurrying in, driven by a friend from Cambridge where he had just finished his Law degree finals. We had been unable to contact Henry immediately – he was at the Kent County Show, but had not heard the public-address call for him – but he turned up later. I have to say they were marvellous, straight away establishing a roster for visiting so there would always be one of us at the bedside, and creating the positive attitude that was to carry us through the upheavals of the next months.

I do not remember much more of that evening,

except that we asked to spend the night there, in a waiting room.

Glenn Neil-Dwyer FRCS (neurosurgeon)

When my bleeper went around midday on 3 June 1977, the switchboard told me a girl out riding in Kent had had a fall, there was suspected brain damage, and we'd accepted transfer to the Brook Hospital.

As Regional Neurosurgical Consultant at the Brook, this was nothing new to me. Even since the compulsory wearing of hard riding hats, with all the horse activity in our area we would have two or three cases a month like this.

Georgina Colthurst, in deep coma, went straight into our Jefferson Ward intensive care unit. From the bruising on her left cheek and the spontaneous jerking of her right arm and leg, it seemed there was pressure on her brain on the left side, inside the cranium. The ward sister was just finishing shaving away the thick, long dark hair on that side.

We put a collar on her in case of fractured neck vertebrae before she was wheeled off to X-ray, and then to the brain scanner.

Brain damage is always tricky to diagnose and correspondingly difficult to treat. With most other trauma you have clear signs and symptoms, and you can work to head off developing problems. With fractures, you set the bones and apply splints, with fevers you administer therapeutic drugs, and with haemorrhaging you block off and stitch up.

27

But almost always with brain damage, you can't see what's wrong, or at any rate not clearly enough to take immediate action. It's been likened to driving in fog so dense you can't see even the kerbside.

I don't like the term 'passive care', because that implies nothing much is actually done, but it does apply here because the right care is rarely, in the usual sense of the word, active. However, and in a *positive* sense, we have to watch and wait, and then act only when we're certain we'll do good, and not harm. And what is seldom realised here is the degree of nursing skill required: not only does literally everything have to be done for the patient, often up to life support itself, but also the most meticulous records must be kept of everything he or she does or does not exhibit. There are half-hourly (or more frequent) monitorings of blood pressure, temperature, pulse and respiration, and the more mundane things like trimming hair and nails, and the protection of eyes – everything, all day and all night, often for weeks and months on end. Keeping the airway open and maintaining the vigil for adverse signs are just the start. Neurological care is the most demanding of all nursing, and it requires dedication from a very special kind of person. At the Brook our department was particularly well served.

With Georgina, we had X-rays and a scan which showed no skull or neck fractures, but there was definite brain swelling, and even while I was assessing that, the stimuli we were administering to judge the state of her brain functions – essentially, needle pricks to parts of her limbs – began ringing up the warnings. First, she just flinched away – the voluntary removal from pain. So far, so good. Then, as we watched, her right arm began to flail out of control. That meant a big drop in her condition, and I became concerned even as, to the next stimulus, her whole body spasmed and went rigid.

This is called decerebrate movement, and it's caused by the deprivation of all links with the larger part of the brain. So Georgina's brain's lower, smaller region – by the spinal cord and the central nervous system – was all that was working. She had only to lose *that* link and she would be dead. We had to move quickly.

I followed her into theatre, gowned and scrubbed up and at 3 pm drilled two small holes – we call them burr holes – in her cranium to relieve pressure from what could have been a blood clot just inside the cranium. But no clot was evident – no blood emanated from the shaven head. So, it was probably the continued swelling of bruised tissue that was pulling her down, and that meant intravenous fluids, and steroid-type drugs to arrest the swelling. We administered these and a catheter straight away, but more we could not – dared not – do. From here we had to wait. Watch, and wait.

And back in the ward an hour later, to our relief, she began to lose some pallor, and slowly to make little limb movements – nothing dramatic, but spontaneously, restlessly . . . so, the brain was at least functioning again. We weren't out of the wood – unlike other bruised body tissue, a damaged brain often goes on swelling more and more for days – but we'd met the immediate challenge.

To the public, a surgeon seems detached from his patients, and that impression is entirely correct. People are subjectively concerned with their relatives and friends, and I'm objectively concerned with my job. It has to be that way, and for that reason few surgeons will operate on people close to them. Involvement in a stressful personal situation doesn't make for balanced judgment.

So you keep your distance. Of course you are sympathetic, but with 15,000 patients a year, there's only so much to go round. Inevitably you forget patients and relatives and circumstances as the days and weeks carry them out of your care and, you hope, back to their normal lives.

But the Colthursts tend to stay in one's memory for a number of reasons.

Georgina herself was, on admission and even in coma, unusual. Very tall – almost six feet – and, despite the shaved and bruised head, clearly of considerable beauty; she was also, to a doctor's eye, splendidly fit. Her muscle tone was excellent, and her injuries notwithstanding, her pulse and heart rate were almost normal, and indeed this fitness – through her riding, swimming, games-playing and so on – was, and was to be, of great importance.

And then there was the family. They descended on Jefferson Ward to become a support system unique in my experience. Her father impressed as a big man in every sense: where his presence could have been physically intimidating, instead what came over was his total dedication to one thing: the rehabilitation of Georgina. Nothing, but nothing, was too much trouble – hours without end behind the wheel along the thirty miles between their home and the Brook, or the twenty miles from his City office, a daily total of a hundred miles, all in London's peak traffic periods, each and every day. And then his goodwill and optimism – to the extent that our staff began to wonder at such sheer energy as the weeks went by – seemed to well from some boundless source.

Her brothers, too, showed that they just didn't see Georgina's defeat as an option. There was always one of them at her bedside, smartly suited either on the way to or returning from his work or studies in law, medicine or languages, and often all three, and quite often with friends as well. Their aim was to keep up a kind of audio-subliminal flow of sound familiar to their sister, and their repertoire seemed limitless: spirited talk, and card and board games such as Monopoly and draughts played actually on her supine form, and sounds they'd taped of home – from horses in the stables, and favourite pop songs, and school friends' messages, to hounds at their local hunt kennels – and even dabbing her perfume on her cheeks. And they'd hold unending conversations with her, of course one-way but always directing questions to and phrasing answers from her, just as though she had been momentarily lost for words.

But I think it was her mother I remember best. A lady of profound courage, she became the fundamental influence in Georgina's weeks with us. In that quiet presence always at Georgina's bedside, the consistency of caring and bravery, forcing hope forward in the face of despair, I found very moving.

And indeed, the prognosis was looking promising and we had begun to relax when, suddenly on the ninth day, everything changed.

James Colthurst (brother)

I was in a difficult position over Georgina's accident.

At the precise time, in June 1977, at the end of my second-year medical studies at St Thomas's Hospital, I suppose I knew rather more than the average person about her condition, and also regarding the prognosis and management of it. But I wasn't qualified, and so I could not expect anyone to take what I said seriously: as medical students say – no white coat, no vote.

This fact hit me even as my parents were telling me on the phone that George – as we brothers called her – was in the Brook Neurological Ward, in deep coma.

Dad insisted there was nothing to be done for her by us that evening. They were going to break the news to Henry and then stay the night at the hospital. Charles had been there, and had gone back to Cambridge to pack his things.

I stacked my books away – I was at the start of that year's exams – and ran down to the car to set off home through the heavy south London traffic. I inched my way through the Elephant and Castle and New Cross, and then along the A2, and across Blackheath and over the roundabout at the other side to the long, open up-gradient and the red-brick walls of the Brook. It was more or less my usual route home anyway, but I was to get to know every single inch of it in the next two months.

It was a dreadful time. We had to face the fact that, according to the prognosis at the Brook, Georgina had a fifty-fifty chance of living.

I drove to the hospital the next morning. In her bed, in the most critical station outside the sister's office, George looked as I'd expected, and then not so. I'd seen patients in head injury coma of course, but I suppose nothing can prepare you for it in someone really close.

She lay absolutely still, half-bald head lolling on the pillow, face chalky grey, with a huge mottled bruise on her left cheek. Her eyes stared up at us, and through us. Then as I watched, her arms and legs twitched faintly, once or twice, and were still. Then they twitched again, and were still again. It was the involuntary way it was happening that most got through to me. It was her, and yet it wasn't her. Something else in her was doing this.

And we were powerless.

There was nothing to do except sit and watch and wait.

In the next few days we established a strategy with the aim of having as many of us as possible at Georgina's bedside, for as long as possible. We talked with Mr Neil-Dwyer, Georgina's neurosurgeon, and among other things he impressed on us the importance of subliminal therapy, of familiar sounds around her all the time – family conversation, and things recorded from home-like noises from the yard, and people she knew, so when we tired of talking we could switch on the tapes. He was tremendously helpful, and not at all put out by this sudden avalanche of Colthursts setting up home in his ward.

So the next few days established a routine, and I managed to keep revising for each afternoon's exams by leaving Lambeth after an early breakfast and spreading my books and files all over Georgina and her bedside furniture – and of course Mum was there, all day and every day, permanent and reassuring as a rock. Then around midday I'd pack up and drive off to Lambeth and the exam room, and then back down to Blackheath in the evening.

Mr Neil-Dwyer had warned that if a crisis should come, it would most probably be at the end of the first week. So we breathed several quiet sighs of relief when 10 June came and went with nothing untoward happening.

And then, the following day, it happened.

Mum and Dad decided to risk a morning off for

various urgent things down in Kent. I had no exams – it was a Saturday – and so I said I'd spend the whole day at the Brook, and get into solid revision.

At eleven o'clock I drove out of the gates and up Crockham Hill towards London, thinking more of Monday's exams than anything else, and fairly soon I was passing through the Saturday morning traffic.

At that minute, a Brook nursing sister was dialling our home.

I breezed into the ward around midday to see Mr Neil-Dwyer and three nurses craning over Georgina's bed – at 11.20 they'd suddenly been recording drops in the instruments' readings – respiration from her normal 18 a minute, to 16; pulse from a steady 80 to 70, and then 60. Blood pressure was the thing they were watching then, because if the BP drops, then so does the blood – and therefore oxygen – supply to the brain. And that was falling too, from 120 to 115, and then 110 . . .

They started wheeling her out to the brain scanner. I asked if I could use the phone, but they'd already called Kent. I snatched another look at the charts. Everything had dropped further: respiration down to 10 – half the required rate. Pulse right down to 48 – again, half what was wanted. And her BP had hit a low of 100 . . .

Charles had gone back to Cambridge. I got the Magdalene lodge porter on the phone and asked him to get a message to my brother as soon as possible. Just the one sentence: Georgina was getting worse.

Then something happened which is, in retrospect, still rather strange.

I felt anger flowing through me. Anger at the situation, at circumstances. And that suddenly changed to anger at George herself, lying there before me dying . . . giving up . . . *dying*, in front of my eyes . . .

'You *aren't* to give up!' I heard myself shouting. 'This is *it*!' I took her hand and began squeezing it. 'This is *it*! You've used up all your options. You've had your chance to die, days ago. That's *gone*! YOU ARE TO HANG ON!'

The other people all down the ward – those who were awake, and the nurses – must have heard every word and been watching, but I don't remember any of that and I wouldn't have cared anyway. She was slipping from me. The fury built and built and I poured it out to the still form, *willing* myself to get through to her . . .

The numbers were still dropping, and somewhere along the line Mr Neil-Dwyer arrived and Mum and Dad came hurrying in, and then the nurses were clustered round, pumping in more steroids, and Manitol to arrest the swelling. Neil-Dwyer was very still. Looking up at him, I knew he was weighing the next option, and that was as critical as it could be. If her respiration and BP dropped further, her brain would be starved of blood, and then of oxygen. The solution would be to give pure oxygen, but to do that she'd have to be sedated, and her reactions would be lost to the monitors, and to us. Then, he'd be

working without reference, in a kind of vacuum . . . I
took George's hand again and Dad took the other,
and we started together. I remember saying again
that this was *it*. And again I told her she'd *had* her
chance to die, and that had *gone* . . . she *had* to keep
going . . . and Dad was telling her there was no other
way, she just *had* to pull herself through and *do* it, for
herself – we'd run out of ideas and solutions, and it
was absolutely and entirely down to *her* . . .

Glenn Neil-Dwyer

Towards evening, Georgina's eyes began to lose
fixed dilation.

That was the first good sign.

The family was extraordinary. They sat all round
her, holding her hands, simply willing her to pull
through.

And, as we watched, the readings began slowly to
move back up. Respiration was climbing from 10 to
12, and then 13 . . . 14, while the pulse rallied and
moved . . . 42 . . . 47 . . . 50. The minutes crawled by
as we watched and talked to her. BP was fluctuating,
but the underlying movement was again upward –
105, 104, 107 as the pulse got stronger, then 106,
109 . . .

It was a remarkable recovery, from what for most
would have been the end, and I am sure that as well
as Georgina's splendid physical condition, and the
young brain, and the steroid counter-swelling
therapy, it was due as much to the vitality of the

family's exterior stimuli; by that mid-evening they were still all crowded round the bed in a sort of tableau of wills, all concentrated on the central supine figure of Georgina, talking, urging, encouraging, almost physically forcing her to pull through . . . Certainly, a magnificent picture of family unity. I remember in particular James insisting: 'Don't go – we're here, all round you. You'll be all right, you'll be fine . . . you are *not* to give up . . .'

Later that evening, I felt I could tell them the worst was over: the read-outs showed respiration back to 20, pulse and BP steady at 80 and 120, and there was even the odd little twitching movement in her limbs.

Before I left that night, I told the ward sister to put back the naso-gastric tube, and the required calories in fats and salts began again to flow into the patient.

For the next two weeks we were on a fairly typical plateau for the type of injury – treating a mild chest infection (probably from the tube feeding) and administering the EEG (electroencephalogram) to assess damage, and response quality to arousal, with excellent results.

She was of course still at the acute stage, deeply unconscious and restless, with the left side still exhibiting weakness, but on the morning of 16 June one of the nurses suddenly asked her to move her right leg – and, she did.

This was for us a big breakthrough, as I explained to the parents. But I could see they were disappointed at there being no more than that to show.

And still, there was hardly a moment from dawn to dusk when the mother wasn't there, and almost invariably one or more of the brothers and the father each and every evening.

Four days later our neurophysiologist administered a further EEG and was able to tell the family that there was still some improvement.

Then, a couple of days after that, I decided we were ready to give the family as full a prognosis as we could.

Seated with them at Georgina's bed, I said: 'This is the situation. First, she's quite clearly improving. But, I cannot predict with certainty when or even if she will again function quite normally. It could well happen, but we can't at this stage be sure. I would put the chances at 75–25 in her favour, at the present moment.'

Her father began to look very concerned indeed, but I went on: 'In these things we have to expect – expect, but not take for granted – that when she should regain full consciousness, her behaviour might be, at least at first, rather erratic: moods, memory and concentration difficulties, and her intellectual performance may be impaired.'

'What can be *done*?' he insisted.

'Basically, we must wait and see what the signs and symptoms are, before we're able to decide,' I said. 'There's much that *could* be done, but we can't treat a condition until it manifests itself. And the other area for consideration – not for worry, but for consideration – is her left side, the return to normal

strength and movement in her left arm and left leg.
Again, there is enormous potential for physiotherapy,
but when we start that, it will take time.'

And in fact, regarding the left arm in particular,
there was something else on my mind. The brain
injury had caused a spasm in Georgina's left arm.
The condition is known as spasticity, where the
muscles involved become rigid. This had set her
arm, folded in a V at the elbow, across her chest.

Any mechanical disturbance of spasticity creates
calcification in the muscle tissue: that is, the blood
deposits calcium as a reactive defence mechanism,
so immobilising the area – in Georgina's case the left
elbow – further. It's a form of natural splinting.

Through an unfortunate misunderstanding, one
of Georgina's nurses had straightened that left arm
to take her blood pressure, so disturbing the
spasticity, and thereby creating calcification around
the elbow.

Thus, as early as possible, we had to investigate a
physiotherapy programme to promote blood flow in
the left arm, to carry the calcium away.

Then, Georgina's parents asked if I would mind a
second opinion.

George Bernard Northcroft MBE FRCS *(neurosurgeon)*

It has been said that my time as an 8th Army Desert
Rat – I was operating in No 1 Mobile Neurosurgical
Unit in the Western Desert from Alamein and

Tobruk onwards – has afforded me more experience in brain damage than most.

I don't think I would dispute that. Daily occurrences were such as a soldier with his head crushed into sand under a three-ton truck who recovered perfectly after I'd treated him in Cairo; and another patient with half his head shot away and paralysed down one side whom I helped also, and who went on to be a brilliant High Court judge.

One day in the summer of 1977 Glenn Neil-Dwyer phoned me to say a patient's relatives had asked for a second opinion. As Regional Consultant Neurosurgeon I was quite used to such requests: contrary to popular belief, specialists like him are rarely affronted by them – they more usually ask for the views of colleagues in advance of anyone else, in fact.

To give a little background on a neurosurgeon's work as it applies here, probably most is concerned with cerebral contusion, or the bruised brain.

A typical cause of contusion is the shearing strain from rotation of the lower part of the brain against the upper. The brain is shaped like a mushroom: twist the top away from the stem, and we have the picture. This naturally distorts or breaks fibres and destroys cells, so cutting off stimuli to the cortex, or the upper part of the mushroom. Normally the degree of twisting dictates the severity of the condition. Severe shaking of the brain has the same effect. Both bring coma or deep unconsciousness, and possibly death.

Perhaps strangely, severe head wounds do not necessarily have this effect. A man may be shot right through the head and not even be knocked out – and I've seen this – because there may have been little or no twisting. My soldier friend under the three-ton truck stayed wide awake right through the bone healing and full rehabilitation because the crushing had not had any twisting effect.

Deep coma is invariably dangerous, but if the patient survives the first two weeks – and we usually feel the eighth or ninth day is the critical time – the prognosis is generally quite good, and particularly with a young brain and a fit body.

Which brings us to Georgina Colthurst, and Glenn Neil-Dwyer's requested second opinion. I first saw her as yet another girl suffering after a riding accident. That is far from uncommon: riding head injuries are more numerous and serious than, for example, in professional boxing. And oddly enough I already knew of Georgina through her riding expertise, because my own daughter was at the time at St Michael's – in the same year as one Anneka Rice, as a matter of fact.

I was told of Georgina's ninth-day crisis, and I quite agreed with Neil-Dwyer's subsequent diagnosis: it was a condition we term sub-dural haemorrhaging, or bleeding deep in the *dura mater* region of the brain. We believed a vein there had been ruptured, and the issuing blood had exacerbated the general swelling.

It seemed the rupture had since healed, and her

condition correspondingly stabilised.

I understood absolutely the family's anxiety for a definitive prognosis, as did my colleague, and I had the anticipated difficulty in persuading them that these things just cannot be hurried. You can only wait to see how the patient progresses.

In such cases I have to state the obvious: some unconscious patients recover quickly because the damage isn't severe, but invariably, the longer they are in coma, the worse the condition. As Georgina had been deeply unconscious for three weeks, and the general lower limit for severe head injury is seven days, we couldn't expect miracles. That fall had twisted her brain badly. Only time would tell to what extent.

Although she'd clearly lost some brain cells – destroyed forever from the moment of impact – the human brain has a remarkable ten times more cells, and fibres, than it ever needs (the same applies to the liver and kidneys), and so there were plenty left to take over from those gone.

As to treatment, that would be 95 per cent nursing, and nursing of the highest quality. Indeed, only 3 per cent of all head injuries go to theatre to save life: good nursing is the thing, so that problems are not exacerbated.

Neurological nursing has to be of the best because it's so repetitive and demanding and comprehensive, and often so plainly fundamental, and usually all at once, all the time. If chest or bladder or bowel trouble – all typical peripheral head-injury problems – are not detected and treated early, the patient becomes debilitated, loses strength, deteriorates and may consequently die of trauma unrelated to the brain damage. Such basics as keeping a good airway open must be checked and re-checked several times an hour, and day and night, because without air and therefore without oxygen, life ceases, and it first ceases in the brain, and it would happen so much more quickly if the brain were damaged.

After a few weeks and several more visits, we could see a definite improvement in Georgina, and when she began to recognise people, and to swallow her own food, and generally continue her recovery, I felt I could bow out, knowing she was in the best hands.

My lasting impression of Georgina Colthurst is as much of the parents and brothers as of the young lady herself. Always at her bedside, their support and concern were quite extraordinary, and it was gratifying to see such a staunch and devoted family unit acting in harmony and concert in their daughter and sister's cause.

James Colthurst

We kept throwing ideas at each other on how to develop Glenn Neil-Dwyer's recommended subliminal therapy, the indirect absorption by the patient of information and stimuli to help the brain start functioning again.

I think there were four of us in the hospital at the time, playing cards on George's body as a table, and running the 'Horse and Hound' tapes, as we called them, in the hope that she would hear something familiar, when Dad suddenly said: 'Why don't we bring Tiny and Snoopy up here? And the dogs, while we're at it?'

Like a lot of good ideas, it seemed amazing that we had not thought of it before.

So next day the Oakley box trundled up from Kent with the two little greys in the back and Tish and Susie hopping about in the cab with Mum and Dad, excited as only fox terriers can be. I doubt if anybody at the Brook will ever forget that day.

Henry and I had quite enjoyed making the 'Horse and Hound' tapes, although there was a lot of work involved. We had put together some sounds of home life, particularly outdoor noises such as horses snickering and dogs barking and it must be said that we'd had some success with these at the Brook: George's restlessness calmed when we switched them on, and a sort of attentiveness seemed to come over her.

But the visit itself was of course the real thing.

Dad phoned from downstairs and George was propped into her wheelchair, her lolling head supported by a couple of pillows, and we rolled her out to the lift and down to the steps by the car park.

Nurses and staff clustered at the windows overlooking the parking area as Mum and Dad dropped the ramp and led the ponies out, with the dogs cavorting under everyone's feet.

When they brought the little greys over, it was really quite moving. They both nuzzled George with tremors running down their flanks, and Tiny, the older of the two, sidled uncomfortably and tried to get closer as I rested George's good hand on his muzzle.

She herself seemed to be listening for something as I stroked the hand across their necks and cheeks, and Snoopy nudged the left arm, the one locked in a V across her chest, exactly as if he knew there was something wrong there. The two dogs had quietened: Susie sat at George's feet, head cocked, looking up at her; Tish moved restlessly round the chair, to put her forepaws up on the top of the wheel and push her nose up to be stroked.

George says today she has some vague memory of the whole happening, and she did have that attentive, calm aspect as with the tapes, when the ponies were standing before her.

Nevertheless, we agreed after about a quarter of an hour that she'd had enough. There was a sense of anticlimax. I suppose in our hearts we'd been hoping for something more dramatic: not for her to leap from her chair and spring up for a ride, but possibly for greater recognition from those glazed eyes in that stiff, stricken face.

Lady Colthurst

After spending nearly seven weeks in the Jefferson Ward at the Brook, the routine became very familiar to us all. As far as I can remember, after the first night, my husband and I only spent one night there when Georgina was so ill on the ninth day, and that night was spent mainly by her bedside with short intervals trying to sleep on the floor in the adjoining sitting-room.

When we first saw her there, she was among about twenty head-injured patients under intensive care, in the place reserved for the most seriously ill. Gradually she was moved further up the ward, which filled us with hope.

Having rushed through most of the work at home, I used to try and get to the hospital about noon to spend the rest of the day there. As Georgina was unconscious, we were allowed in at any time – in fact encouraged to be there to try to stimulate her. For the first two weeks she was fed through a tube, so meals were not exactly exciting, but as she improved, she began to eat normal hospital meals, and much to our surprise ate everything with some relish, even food she would normally not have touched. We wondered if she had lost her sense of taste; when Nurse Wendy asked what her favourite food was, our response was ice cream and she suggested we should bring some. After the first mouthful Georgina opened her mouth as far as possible for it, obviously appreciating a delicacy she really enjoyed. It then became part of her daily diet.

She was given physio every day by a marvellous man called Tom. On meeting him you would never have thought he was totally blind, as he knew exactly where everyone was in the ward and who they were after initially meeting them. He used to exercise Georgina's limbs and then, with the help of a nurse, walk her round the ward.

After two weeks or more, we were asked to bring her clothes to the ward as it was supposed to be morale-lifting for unconscious patients to be dressed and make them feel more normal. It seemed strange to us with Georgina showing no signs of recovery, but we were told her coma was lightening. She had lost a tremendous amount of weight and become very skinny.

We got to know all the patients in the ward very well during those weeks and chatted to them from time to time. The routine was almost as well known to us as to the nurses, with doctors and surgeons paying regular visits as well as the cheerful Cockney tea-lady. The days were long and tiring without any apparent improvement, and we just hoped for some noise and recognition from our daughter.

Richard used to join me in the hospital after work at about five o'clock, and then we stayed there till eight o'clock every evening, with one or other of the boys often coming in for a time too. We had snacks in the hospital canteen.

After more than six weeks the ward had to be redecorated and patients moved, so it was decided to send Georgina up to St Thomas's. The evening before she left we were both there and I suggested to Richard he let her try and blow his whistle. We gave it to her and said 'blow' – and to our enormous delight and surprise, she did. After this I made various childish noises for her to copy and gradually these sounds came out in a very croaky deep voice from her obviously very rusty voice-box. It was a tremendous step forward – her first words, if words they can be called, for nearly seven weeks. We went home that night greatly encouraged and ready to meet her next morning at St Thomas's. During all our time at the Brook Hospital, we realised how lucky she was to have such marvellous and devoted nursing attention.

Georgina was taken up to St Thomas's by ambulance, accompanied by Nurse Wendy. When we arrived she was asleep in her room on the top floor of the hospital with a marvellous view of the Houses of Parliament across the river. Gradually she opened her eyes and seemed to know us and said our names, and then other short words were repeated. I then asked her what she could see out of the window, hardly daring to hope she would take in what we were saying. To our great joy a very deep voice responded, 'Big Ben,' which seemed to us to mean that the old brain was beginning to function a little again after its long rest. Despite being very confused as to where she was and why, she immediately gave the names of any friends and relatives who came to see her. She had a television in her room and the International Horse Show was on that week. She watched the jumping and knew the names of all the horses and riders.

To us this was another leap forward and a great spur after those long weeks of silence. Apart from her many physical handicaps, from then on it was a question of trying to get her short-term memory back – endlessly asking her what had happened ten minutes before, what she had eaten for the last meal, as she forgot things almost instantly.

There were many advantages in being at St Thomas's in the centre of London. My brother James was coincidentally a student at the hospital, so he was able to see me almost as often as he wanted. It was much easier, too, for Dad and Henry to call in on their way to and from work. I was also lucky enough to be given a room to myself. This made little difference to me while I was in no state to differentiate between a small ward and a private room, but it made things easier for my family.

In fact the privacy may have been bad for me. It restricted the amount of activity visible to me, if ever I was on my own. My door was supposed to be open at all times but in fact well-meaning people often shut it, perhaps to confine the dreadful noises I was making, which only had the effect of making me feel more like a prisoner.

The fact is that as soon as I got my voice back, I started to shout and scream. I have since learnt that this is very common in such cases. I hated being in hospital and it was only by shouting that I could try to make this clear. I wanted to go home, and I even thought that if I made enough noise – the only way I could make a nuisance of myself – the hospital would want to send me home.

I am of course writing these words twelve years later, but whatever my state of consciousness was at the time, I am sure that these are the thoughts that actually went through my mind. I hated hospital, despite the loving attention lavished on me, because it symbolised my helplessness. I felt somehow I was being punished, but exactly why and what for I had no idea. Even in my useless condition, I thought that normality would only return if I could go home.

Unfortunately I could not explain this to anybody, not to the doctors, not to the nurses, not to my family. I was only beginning to be able to speak words and make any sort of sensible sentence. In desperation and frustration I resorted to the only thing I was any good at – screaming at the top of my voice. Somebody later told me that I sounded like a howling hyena.

I was angry and confused at my predicament. Why was I not at home, doing my school exams, looking after my ponies and training for the Three-Day Event at Fontainebleau? The minutes seemed to drag by into hours between the nurse coming to the door to look in, to unhook the clipboard from the end of the bed, to take my temperature, blood pressure and pulse, or to help me with my natural functions, or whatever. I hated every single moment of being there and the only way I could protest was by shouting. Unfortunately this resulted in the doctors sedating me, which my father could not understand. He argued that the whole point of my hospitalisation was to get me back to full consciousness, whereas sedation had the opposite effect. What is the point of giving sleeping pills to someone you want to wake up?

Another problem was that I had unbalanced vision which made it very difficult to focus. I also often felt very cold because my circulation had been badly affected by the accident. My body clock was haywire and I did not know if it was morning or afternoon. One side of me seemed not to be functioning at all. None of this helped my frame of mind.

I was dreadfully lonely, confused and isolated. Where was I? Why was I there? Was it a dream, or more likely a nightmare? If so, it was going on too long. I actually thought for a time that I was dead. Had the world blown up perhaps? Was I being punished and in Hell? If so, why? What had I done to deserve this treatment? But if I really were in Hell, why was my family also there, hovering around me? They were good people who should be in Heaven. Perhaps, after all, this was what Heaven was like. But that could not be because if I were in Heaven, I would surely be able to move and not be helpless. I would be able to communicate. I would be happy.

No, this was not Heaven, but just what it was and where I was bewildered me. I felt desperately, frighteningly insecure, and I began to feel terrified, trapped and unable to escape.

I knew that my only release would come from going home. It would be like waking up from a nightmare. It would be an instant passport to normality.

Caroline 'Scruffy' Mooring
(schoolfriend)

I remember 27 July dawning – an exciting, hot Kent
summer day for me.

Outside her family I suppose I'd been as close to
Georgina as anyone – probably because I wasn't
particularly horsey, and so we didn't compete in that
way, but also because we were the biggest tomboys
at St Michael's.

And that day I'd been allowed up to London to see
her in hospital. Her other great pal, Gillian Smith,
and I were going to make a day of it.

I didn't come by my nickname by chance. My
mother would despair of what she called her
two-legged disaster returning each evening, when
in the morning I'd departed so neatly turned out,
from beribboned straw hat and rustling summer
uniform dress to white knee-socks and polished
brown shoes. I couldn't seem to help it: the shoes
just got scuffed climbing trees, the blazer pockets
simply got torn, and I lost count of the bashed-in
boaters I'd try to hide in the hall cloakroom before
my mother saw me.

Of course much of this was through charging
around with Georgina – but not after school, when
she'd whizz off home to gallop away over fences on
Snoopy or Tiny, Tantivy or Folly or whoever was in
for a ride that day, before disappearing for hours to
the tack-room or yard. Horses were her real life. We
– her friends, and in fact most of St Michael's
200-odd students and staff – were pretty pleased

when she came back from France with her second place in the 1976 Pony Club International, and again when she pulled it off at Tidworth the following year, the year we're talking about now, and was shortlisted for the Junior Three-Day Event at Fontainebleau. This did not surprise us because she really worked at her riding and loved every single minute.

The first inkling of something amiss was no Georgina in the crowd the previous month, milling and chatting in the sunshine outside the exam hall at school. It would have been impossible to miss that tall figure with the beautiful long dark hair. You just didn't miss Georgina.

Then there was her desk in the hall, just across the aisle from me, empty and bare, as the rest of us scribbled and frowned and sucked our pens over the answer sheets. I remember it was English Literature that morning.

And as we poured outside for lunch, the bad news was going round quickly, as it does. Georgina had been taken to hospital after a fall.

Next day my mother told me George was extremely ill – she'd been on the phone to the Colthursts, I think – deeply unconscious, and perhaps even in danger of her life.

Anyway, no one except family was allowed near her for several weeks, and by that time I was away in France on the first part of my summer holiday. When we got back we heard George had come round, and I rang Gillian straight away to fix the trip to London and St Thomas's Hospital.

It was fun getting ready for that: we ran into the station only just in time, having dawdled in sweetshops and newsagents to measure our pocket money against what chocolates (soft centres, and marzipan) and magazines she'd like. Looking forward to a good laugh, we grabbed pounds of grapes and pears from the stall in the station approach and just made it as the guard's flag was waving.

Victoria Station is close to Lambeth, so it wasn't long before the lift doors were opening on the corridor for George's ward. That was when we heard the howling.

I don't want to dramatise what happened in the next half hour, but the one thing Gillian and I asked each other over and over again afterwards was: why hadn't someone told us?

Shouting and bellowing was coming through a pair of grey doors as the nurse – I remember she was looking embarrassed and worried – led us in. A figure was lying on the bed, like a long, broken doll. One arm seemed locked across its chest. The eyes in the shaven skull were staring wildly. For seconds, we just didn't recognise her. Then, as we edged over to the bed, the head suddenly swivelled round at us and screeched: 'Who are you? Who are you?'

Another nurse came in to help the first prop the figure up. The eyes were staring at us and all around us, and an incoherent sound started from the straining throat, indicating recognition. We put the magazines and things on the counterpane by the hand at her side, and started to talk to her.

That seemed to calm her a little, and after a couple of minutes she suddenly murmured: 'It's Scruff . . . it's Scruffy . . .' Then she smiled and said: 'Gillian . . . Gillian,' and I told her she ought to look at what we'd brought her.

She glanced down, and then her face contorted and she bellowed, swept her good hand clumsily across the bed and shoved everything off. The magazines fell with a slap, the bags burst and the fruit went rolling everywhere, under the bed and over to the corner basin. She began to ramble, then she suddenly shrieked: 'I want to go home, home . . .' and started to babble and cry and move on the bed.

The nurses must have been waiting outside, because they came hurrying straight in and said they thought we ought to go.

We were both very quiet on the way back to Victoria. All thoughts of the day out had evaporated.

Lady 'Addie' Raeburn (healer)

I would very much like to make one thing clear. I have an inexplicable gift for transferring energy – for want of a better phrase – to others, which thereby helps them to heal themselves. So I describe myself, and only when I have to, simply as a healer – not as a faith-healer, or a medium, or a white (or any other colour) witch, or indeed as anything else.

I don't know how or why I am able to speed up

nature's course, which is what seems to happen, and I do so fairly sparingly because frankly I don't know everything about what I do in this way.

I first heard of Georgina Colthurst through a nephew who rowed at Eton with her brother, James, who had then gone on to his second year as a medical student at St Thomas's Hospital in London. As I lived quite near – my husband was then Governor of the Tower of London – I agreed to help if I could. James cleared the way through hospital protocol: it may have helped that I'd had good results in controlled experiments at Bart's here in London, and at Harvard in the United States, and also that I work elsewhere with conventional medical practitioners.

So, I went to see Georgina in St Thomas's.

I'm quite used to the inside of a hospital ward and the hushed relatives-at-the-bedside scene round the recumbent form. With Georgina it was quite different.

I could hear garbled shouting in the corridor as the lift doors opened. Nurses hurried past. I wondered why there was no sound-proofing.

Through the sideward door there was just one bed, with a long figure under a white counterpane. The eyes were staring and unfocused in a head shaved on one side like a Mohican Indian. From a slack, drooling mouth came the furious howling: 'I want to go home, I want to go home!' like a demented child.

I took her half-shaved head into my hands. The

shuddering slowly subsided, and the eyes stilled,
and in a few seconds they closed quietly. I knew
more or less what was happening because other
patients remembered, as for the first time, feeling
heat or cold, and draughts. What was needed was a
change in the distorted brain rhythms, so that
Georgina could begin to do what was right for
herself . . .

'You know, Addie,' she was to tell me, much later,
'it was absolutely extraordinary. I could feel you,
that first time, and there were those bursts of colour
of amazing intensity behind my eyes.'

Almost imperceptibly the long form gently
extended, in a sort of sleepy stretch.

I don't know how long we were there like that. I
can seldom tell with accuracy. At Bart's when they
had me on an ECG during a similar treatment, my
psyche was apparently operating at three distinctly
delineated levels on the instrument – 'with blips all
over the place'.

When Georgina's breathing was slow and regular,
and she seemed to be sleeping quietly, I spoke for a
few minutes with her family before leaving.

I'm told the bellowing stopped that day after my
visit, but this was no miraculous cure. She still
couldn't walk, her memory was almost non-existent,
she certainly couldn't write anything, and she still had
an enormous appetite and thirst – indeed once, when
a nurse left a bar of soap on her bed table for a
moment, with neither distaste nor relish she
swallowed every last morsel in seconds.

However, she was more physically cohesive, more aware, from then onwards. She could hold a magazine or a spoon with food for a few seconds, and she could sit up for a minute or two without toppling over.

So, it was a small start. But it was a start. And I began to think what might be the best avenues for her eventual rehabilitation.

It would be wonderfully dramatic if I could set down exactly what happened to me during Addie Raeburn's first treatment, but I honestly cannot recall anything in detail. My parents have since told me that they were prepared to try anything to effect a cure. My father had been given a very pessimistic diagnosis about me when I first got to St Thomas's, and although he was told that my prospects were not hopeless, it was indicated that my chances of recovery were not necessarily bright. There was even a danger that I might never walk properly again.

Although he had every faith in the doctors and in particular in the expertise of the staff at St Thomas's, he was determined to leave no avenue unexplored to secure my full recovery. Alternative therapy as a complement to normal medical attention was worth trying. If a witch-doctor had been on hand or a voodoo dancer, I daresay he would have sought their services as an ancillary to those of the medical profession. In fact on the day Lady Raeburn first saw me, a faith-healer had just visited me; but Addie was the first non-medical person to achieve an almost instant success. Apparently she held my head in her hands, and the one thing I can seem to remember is the inside of my head expanding in vivid lights and a sort of jumbled change taking place. It is difficult to describe. I imagined that there were people inside my head, wise people like my dead grandfather, giving me advice. I felt that they were there to guide me, that if I asked them for help they would tell me what to do. And with this feeling came a sort of peacefulness.

I am told that I fell into a deep sleep and when I awoke my mind seemed to be clearer and lighter. The door opened and someone came quietly to the bed. I could turn my head and saw that it was James. I said something but I don't remember what it was. He was to tell me months afterwards that I croaked: 'That woman . . . she made the gods in my head go wild . . .'

Paradoxically I had come out of this experience more aware than ever and even more determined to escape my prison. Instead of being calmer, I yelled and demanded all the more. My inability to communicate was what frightened me most, and I suppose that is why I screamed so shrilly and insistently. I have since learnt that a head-injured patient comes out of a coma like a baby, and I had to pick up sixteen years' experience in a very short time.

That night, however, I slept, properly and without sleeping pills, for the first time since my accident.

The following morning I was more determined than ever to go home. I simply had to get out of hospital, where there was no incentive for me to recover. This may sound peculiar but that was my feeling. I knew instinctively that returning home would give me the initiative to return to normal. I felt trapped in hospital, and home represented both freedom and security.

Of course I had no idea how dangerously near to death I had been or how serious my condition was. In fact I did not believe that I was ill at all, strange as that may sound. I thought that the real Georgina was somewhere else, and that I was only something to do with her because her family were surrounding me.

I had been utterly bewildered, even terrified, during my time in hospital from the moment I regained sufficient consciousness to be aware of anything. I thought I might be dreaming but it made no difference whether my eyes were open or shut. I could barely move and the only reality I seemed to grasp was that I was not at home. It slowly began to dawn on me that I was in hospital, but I did not at first know why; and when I was told that my horse had fallen, I would not believe it. I was incredibly confused. I did not believe that a horse – a creature I loved – could possibly be responsible for my helpless condition, let alone a favourite animal such as Tantivy.

This may tell the reader something about my real condition and state of mind and may explain why the doctors were dead against sending me home, believing that I was not ready to leave hospital and that, if I did, my parents would be utterly unable to cope. They were probably right about my readiness to return home, but they seriously underestimated my parents.

My father had already persuaded the hospital to take me off the sleeping pills and now my mother courageously made the decision to take me home. The arrangement was that I should return to St Thomas's after a trial weekend at home, which the doctors probably thought would be a trying weekend for my parents, who no doubt would want to return me thankfully to the hospital's care on the Monday morning. In any case I had to see a psychologist at the hospital early in the week.

I remember being propped into a wheelchair and rolled out down the corridor, into the lift and out to my father's car. I was going home. Everyone except the family said it was too soon, but I did not care. It was a beautiful, sunny morning. Home was where I was going and home was where I intended to stay. I suspect too that my mother had no intention of returning me to St Thomas's unless it was absolutely necessary.

I weighed just over four stone. My left side was completely paralysed, with my arm bent to my right shoulder, and of course I could not walk or do anything for myself. Nevertheless my return home was the first practical step in getting back.

I never did return to the hospital except to see the psychologist. He showed me pictures of old film stars and asked me if I recognised them. They were so old, and of such a different generation, that it was not surprising that I only recognised Fred Astaire.

Of course my return home was far sooner than normal in my circumstances, but I am blessed with a loving, capable and sensible family. The first thing my mother said to me was: 'Remember, you're not to shout. If you make a noise, what will the neighbours think?' This was all that was necessary to keep me in order. I still had a very long way to go, however, and for quite some time I thought I was four years old and greeted my next achievement by celebrating my fifth birthday. I had gradually to grow up again to my actual age of sixteen. For a long time I had to be treated like a little baby because there was nothing I could do for myself.

James was at home that weekend and helped to carry me up and down stairs. Just as my father had refused a 'disabled' sticker for his car, saying that would be tempting fate, so he refused to bring a bed downstairs for me, saying: 'If you start sleeping downstairs, you'll end up sleeping downstairs.'

In my confused state, I stupidly thought that I would return to complete normality the minute I got back to the family house. Even during the car journey, I had expected some dramatic improvement in my condition with every mile, but the reality was that I was becoming exhausted, and when nothing very much seemed to happen, I became more and more depressed.

I had realised with a shock when we went through the wrought-iron gates at the end of our drive that I was no better than when I left hospital. I had been expecting a miracle and it had not happened. But there was one solid crumb of comfort. I might have changed but the house and its surroundings were the same as ever. I was back on familiar territory.

I was too tired, however, to take it all in, and had to be put immediately to bed. It annoyed me that I had to be carried up the stairs to my bedroom. I had fantasised that, on return home, I would have regained the power of my legs. I was sufficiently aware, though, that the position of my bed had been changed. I did not know why at the time, but of course there were good, practical reasons.

I was so pleased to get into my own bed. I was ready to fall asleep almost before my head touched the pillow, but I remember not wanting to sleep until I had looked around. I now thought that I would return to normal as soon as I saw the ponies. That afternoon, soon after I woke up, I was carried downstairs and outside to the wheelchair, in which I was taken up the drive and round to the stables. I was elated in the sure knowledge that seeing Tiny and Snoopy would immediately complete my rehabilitation. Tiny in particular had always helped me when I was unwell. In fact I have always called him Dr Tiny because if ever I had a bruise or a cold, he seemed to make it better.

I was really pleased to see the ponies and they were obviously thrilled to see me. Each had a different way of showing it. Snoopy sniffed me all over and nuzzled my body. Tiny kissed me on my face in the special way he had. They must have been puzzled as to why I was in a wheelchair and in such a contorted shape. I was very happy of course until I realised that I was still a useless invalid.

I fell back on another line of defence, telling myself that I would be cured after a really good night's sleep in my own bed at home, but I woke up in the morning unchanged. So I then told myself that all would be well again after I had sat on Tiny. I was able to make it clear to everyone that this is what I wanted to do. Despite my family's concern, they realised how important this was to me and soon after breakfast, my wish was granted.

I had no coordination or balance, my left side was still paralysed and my left arm was out of commission, so I had to be placed on the pony's back and supported on either side. All we did was walk a few paces because I was

1a Aged nine months, with my mother, November 1961.

1b With my brothers (from the bottom) James, Henry and Charles, 1967.

2a On our first pony, Dolly, in Ireland, 1966.

2b Driving Clover with Foxy Mac, Ireland, 1966.

3a Blarney Castle, owned by my family.

3b At Wheatlands with my ballet cup, 1967.

4a With Tiny at the Buxted Show, 1967.

4b With Tiny at the Old Surrey and
Burstow Pony Club Hunter Trials, 1969.

5a On Snoopy (Silver Streak), being presented with First Prize in the Working Hunter Pony Championships at Peterborough, 1972.

5b On Oberon, with Deirdre Robinson, winning the pairs competition at the Arab Performance Show, Salisbury, 1971.

6a On Witch (Dancing Surprise), winning second place in the sidesaddle competition at the Royal International Horse Show, Wembley, 1972.

6b On Tantivy (the horse I was riding when I had my accident) at the Reigation Horse Show, placed first in the Surrey Novices, 1975.

7a Minnie's famous helicopter jump
at the Pony Club Horse Trials at Stoneleigh, 1974.

7b On Folks Folly, winning first place
in sidesaddle jumping, Hickstead, 1977.

8a & **b** Coming second on Minnie in the Junior International Pony Club Three-Day Event at Fontainbleau, 1976.

incredibly weak. Even my mother, who knew how keen I was to sit on Tiny, was surprised when I asked to get off after no more than five minutes.

I was still virtually helpless, and it was then that I realised that no miracle cure was available and that I would have to work long and hard to rehabilitate myself.

The re-learning process was not as I had anticipated. I had to re-learn every everyday skill. As my physical condition improved and I became stronger, I had to discover how to walk again. At first I could not stand at all on my own two feet. I used to haul myself around with my right arm around my brother James's neck, with his arm around my waist.

I had to re-learn how to eat; not just how to cut things up, but how to push bits on to a fork, and how to get that fork to, and then into, my mouth. I remember taking a whole peach from a friend and shoving it into my mouth, stone and all!

I had to learn how to drink from a cup and hold a saucer. I had to learn how to dress myself, and how to write, how to wash and bathe, and of course go to the loo. I was almost a skeleton and such a bag of skin and bones that I could not have managed had James not padded a special seat for me with foam.

I had to learn to focus, for I was seeing double some of the time. It was not easy to think and my powers of concentration were practically nil. I had to learn to use my hands. I tried once to pick up a pencil with my good right hand but it rolled out of my fingers and on to the floor.

My long-term memory was better than my short-term, and attempts to improve it had started at St Thomas's. For example I had been encouraged to watch the Royal International Horse Show at Wembley on the television, and the following day I was questioned about who had won the previous day. I got the placings all jumbled up to begin with, although I always knew the personalities involved. Back at home, I was asked who had visited me the day before, what I had had for meals and what I had done. My memory gradually improved.

I had no control over thirst or hunger and I was inclined to eat and drink to excess. No one knew if I really needed so much nourishment but as I was so thin, no one wanted to deprive me of the liquids and solids I incessantly demanded. Everybody erred on the lenient side.

I had completely to re-discipline myself. It was very important to learn to express myself intelligently and to speak understandably. Later I had to adjust to social normalities, such as keeping my temper and considering others.

Most of the required skills were necessary each and every day and sometimes several times each day. They demanded constant practice and repetition and a monotonous curriculum. I had to start virtually from scratch and I often failed, which caused me quite desperate depression. One of the best therapies was visiting Dr Tiny in his stable. I always felt better afterwards.

Of course I could not have managed without my family, but my brothers' urging and cajoling, and their encouragement, sometimes seemed to me close to bullying. It was hard to tolerate, especially when my mind did not know how to tolerate. Life just did not seem fair.

I suppose my family's efforts worked rather like brainwashing. I knew everything was for my own good and that everyone, myself included, had only one aim in mind – my complete recovery – but the effort was sometimes not easy to accept and I felt frustrated, angry and despairing.

I admit that I have never had much patience. My parents however displayed very great patience, and made considerable sacrifices for my benefit. My father actually slept on a mattress at the side of my bed for several weeks. He did not want me to be alone at night. He was always on duty in case I needed to go to the loo, for example, or in case I fell out of bed!

One night, two or three days after my return home, I took him by surprise. I was determined to prove myself, perhaps because I was terrified of being returned to hospital. I had had a strange dream that I was completely back to normal. When I awoke, I believed that this dream was telling me something, that I was ready to take a positive step towards establishing my improvement. Under its influence, I actually managed to stand up on my own with the help of my bedside table and bed. I felt rock solid. I looked at my father, who was asleep. 'Look at me,' I said twice before he heard me. Still drowsy, he ordered me sternly to sit down, whereupon I said, 'Shouldn't you congratulate me?' 'Why?' he asked. 'Because I'm standing,' I shouted.

It was a long process to get back to anything like normal. If I had known then what I know now, how long and hard a path I had to ride, I would have found it much more difficult to face.

Progress was painfully slow. It was not so difficult to recall my childhood, but recent events were all muddled in my mind. One faculty I had not lost was the ability to recognise people, even those I had not seen for a long time. I was asleep one day in the garden when Juliet Nichols turned up unexpectedly. She had been chef d'équipe when I had come second in France in the Pony Club Three-Day Event two years earlier. My parents were surprised that I recognised her at once.

It is astonishing what my brain could and could not do. On the plus side, I could remember people's phone numbers and car number plates with surprising facility. My real problem was one of concentration. I could not deal with any one thing for any length of time. My handwriting was awful. At first my brain would not communicate with my hands, and the effort to coordinate was altogether too much for me. I actually fell asleep in the middle of my first scribble.

Everybody recognised, however, that my span of concentration was greater when it came to the horses. I had more time for them and was happier in their presence. I felt more secure and sure of myself in their company, or talking about them. My friend Jacky Betts, with whom I had usually ridden before school, of course came to see me. In fact she was brilliant: she came to the house almost every single day. I had helped her with her riding and taught her a lot about horses, and now she more than repaid me by helping me in a similar way. At first, when I was literally immobile, she would come up to my room and sit by the bed, and we would talk and talk. It must have been difficult for her, with my hazy understanding and excitable, shrill voice, but she kept coming back. That was when we started our horse quizzes.

Later, when it would not have been much fun watching me plunging around in the pool or grinding on at the writing table, she arrived when I was resting. Then she would press on again about horses, making me remember or teaching me all over again.

'How many colours of horse are there?' she would ask suddenly. (We would find a quick-fire technique best for jogging the memory.) 'Hurry up!'

'Black, brown, chestnut, bay – '

'One more main one. Come on – what about Tiny and Snoopy?'

'Oh yes – grey.'

'Give me some face markings. Come on!'

'Let me see. On the face, a star is like a diamond between the eyes. A stripe is a line down, from forehead to muzzle. A blaze is really a wide stripe.'

'What's a white face?'

'One like yours.'

'Georgina . . .'

'Everything white, all across the front of the head.'

'Correct. What are the aids?'

'Rider's signals to the horse. Hands, legs and voice are natural. Whips and spurs and martingales are artificial.'

'Good. Now, leg markings. What's the difference between a sock and a stocking?'

'A sock goes halfway up the cannon bone. A stocking – can't remember.'

'Yes, you can. A stocking goes . . .'

'Up to the – the knee?'

'Or hock. Well done. What sort of fence is a trakener?'

'That's easy. A ditch with a rail across it.'

'Very well, clever – an oxer?'

'Easy again. A hedge fence, with rails in front and behind it.'

'Let's get on to stable management questions. What's mud fever?'

'I don't know.'

'Yes, you do.'

'No, I don't.'

'Come on, Georgina. Think.'

But there were some things I just could not recall, and some were quite elementary from early Pony Club days.

'You really don't remember? Well, it's like chapped hands in us humans. If you let a horse's legs and feet get really wet so that the natural oils are drawn off, and don't dry them quickly, then you get inflammation. That's mud fever. Remember now?'

I did, dimly.

'So what's the treatment?'

'Keep the legs dry in the stable, of course. Brush them out as soon as the mud's dried. Vaseline or linseed oil beforehand. Right?'

'Who said she couldn't remember? You mustn't give up.'

'Bossy boots. Come on. Another question. Make it harder.'

'All right. Let's see – are you any good at shoes and shoeing?'

'I hope so.'

'Then what's a feather-edged shoe?'

'That's to stop a horse brushing its legs together.'

'OK. So how does this feather-edged shoe work?'

'Well, the inside edges are thinner and sort of rounded, so it doesn't cut the opposite foot.'

'What a clever-clogs! Well remembered.'

'Next one, please.'

'Right. What does a red ribbon mean when it's in the tail of a horse out hunting?'

'That the horse kicks.'

'Good.'

So we went on, for hours and hours, day after day, getting that part of my memory back. More perhaps than anyone outside my family at this time, Jacky restored my confidence in myself, by involving me in something near to my heart.

My excellent neurosurgeon, Neil-Dwyer, said that riding would be the best therapy. I knew that in any case instinctively. Something told me that as soon as I sat on a pony again, I would return to normal. Of course that was nonsense but in my own mind even sitting for a few moments on Tiny's back, supported on both sides, was the first step back on the long hard road to recovery.

Although all my family are athletic – James for example rowed for Great Britain as a youth international in both eights and coxless fours – and although they all rode in Ireland, it was I who was bitten by the equine bug. I had been taught to skate and swim from an early age and had taken part in athletics at school. I was a good sprinter and simply loved lacrosse. I was also taught to play the piano and I made some progress in ballet classes, in fact won my school's ballet cup.

Of course I did not have time for everything, in addition to my normal schoolwork, and the time came when I had to choose between competing activities. I can remember comparing riding and ballet. In one you are taught to keep your knees in and your heels down, and in the other your knees out and your toes down. I decided I preferred the former! I do not think this will surprise anybody who knew me from the earliest days when I rode Dolly at my grandparents' home in County Kildare, or anyone who had seen me on the leading rein in my first competition at the age of five. I won the class because my father was able to run fast enough for the pony to canter. When the other parents tried, all the riders fell off!

I suppose I could never have opted for any activity other than riding once Tiny came to us. As a child I had been known to say that I was married to him and now I could not have had a more caring friend. All the horses knew that there was something wrong with me and in their individual ways tried their utmost to help. Folly was to become the master helper, but initially it was Tiny who did all he could to make riding easier for me.

Caroline Mooring

After Georgina got home from London, I visited her about twice a week.

I was still pretty wary of what I had seen, though by then she had come on a lot. She was certainly quieter, but she had become simple and child-like – impatient with everything and everyone, and talking in a slurred, high-pitched monotone, just like a little girl being exasperating.

Having been quite painfully thin and underweight, her body beneath her head, bobble-hatted to hide the shaved skull, had become bloated and gross, and ballooned to over 170 lbs – more than twelve stone. That was because of one particular problem: we dared not leave any food or drink – biscuits, fruit, squash, coffee, anything at all – near her, because she would wolf and gulp everything down in seconds. She had lost control over thirst and hunger.

She had lost her dexterity and grace too. It was particularly awful seeing that in someone who had been so fit, and beautiful with it. Now, her shambling walk – just like a jerking boy soldier, I remember – had her sidling along the walls, and hugging the banisters, gasping and groaning with effort.

She mumbled shrilly at me about being unable to dress herself yet and she would snarl in frustration when she could not make her hands do anything, though she had already started on thousands of determined hours to regain her literate skills – reading, talking, and most of all striving to make her hands and mind coordinate to start writing again, fighting her wandering concentration at the same time.

The thing that came over most of all to me, however, was the support of the family. She was never without a brother or parent. I watched them encourage her to climb the stairs to get things, and coax and cajole her through the little skills like tying her laces and dressing herself. Her bewilderment was often heart-rending but she did not resist. That was the thing. She pressed on, hauling on the banisters, or sitting at the table with her face contorted over pen and paper, forcing her hands to try to write. The spidery lines were all over the place, wandering vertically and often right off the page altogether, but she was determined to succeed.

Alongside all of this, she had got back on Tiny, her old grey pony: to begin with, supported on both sides by members of her family. I think the real improvement started from that particular day. She became noticeably more calm and rational from then, and within a week she was walking Tiny round the paddock on her own. I wondered what on earth would happen if she fell off. I thought she was off balance, teetering and swaying in the saddle, frowning hard and trying to keep her left arm from flapping around, as it did almost all the time. But somehow, falling off seemed to be the last thing to mention to anyone there.

Inevitably we began to lose touch as schoolfriends do when they leave school behind. I was working to go up to Oxford and I had already made up my mind to take a look at Australia too, and so I am not really in the picture from the end of the year of the accident. But my lasting memories will be of the sixteen-year-old tomboy with long brown hair flying in the wind as she racketed around the Kent woods with me, and then that empty desk in the exam hall; the ghastly screaming apparition in the grey St Thomas's room, and the shrilly-chattering figure lurching step by step round the walls of

home, or craned fiercely over the table as she willed
her brain to make her hands remember what she
had taught them to do ten and more years
before.

If asked which feeling dominated my convalescence and
rehabilitation, I think I would answer frustration, based on
the fact that I never seemed to improve quickly enough. I
was in despair that there was no instant cure. It was
difficult for me to notice any gradual improvement when I
was looking for some magical change. I raised my own
hopes, only to have them dashed.

There were times when I felt it was so useless to carry on
with so little improvement that I might as well give up. I
remember sitting on my bed and just wishing that I was not
there.

I had no conception at the time of what it meant to
commit suicide – such an idea had never crossed my
youthful, optimistic mind before my accident – but there
was an occasion when I told my parents that I intended to
kill myself. I had not thought it out at all carefully and had
made no actual plan. My practical parents responded quite
calmly because they were used to me coming out with odd
statements when I was feeling particularly depressed. They
asked me what method I would use, and I suddenly
realised that I had no idea. My mother then asked what my
family and friends would do without me. I must admit that I
was not very worried about my friends, some of whom had
apparently disowned me because they were embarrassed by
my condition and change in personality, and it was not

until Mum mentioned the horses that I realised I would have to keep going!

I knew that I was very demanding and I thought that if I got rid of myself, I would be removing a burden from my loving family's shoulders, but they all pointed out to me that my death would increase their burden. They were wonderful in indicating to me what I could not see for myself – that I was making gradual progress.

When I first arrived back home, the family's cheerful optimism fed my own and I regarded my condition as temporary and was hopeful that I would be up and about and back with the horses in no time. It was the middle of the summer holidays too, so there was time to get fit for the autumn school term. I felt as though I was under a spell which would soon be broken, perhaps after a good night's sleep when I would wake up, stop being a bore to everyone, and get right back to being the old Georgina.

It took me some time to realise what a fantasy this was. I was no Sleeping Beauty about to be woken up by some Prince Charming. The horrible reality of my situation dawned slowly as day succeeded frustrating day. My recovery was going to take time, more time, and still more time. It also meant hard work and a monotonous slog. Overcoming one problem, there were always others ahead, and so it went on, with no end in sight.

I was completely off drugs except for Phenobarbitone, which Mr Neil-Dwyer insisted was vital to ward off fits, which would have set me back dreadfully. In fact I had to take the drug in decreasing quantities for about a year. I lived in a sort of haze. I still had uncontrollable thirst and hunger, and my brain and body just would not coordinate, however hard I tried. I had to be helped everywhere. My body clock was upside down – I needed to sleep in the day and I sometimes woke up at two o'clock in the morning, desperate for breakfast. Dad could not have had a very easy time sleeping on the mattress in my room.

I began to believe the real me was not actually inside the useless body that was shaming me. I had always been so capable and active. Now I was confused in body, and worse still in mind. I could not concentrate. I got tired so quickly. I wanted to improve in every way but I kept hitting a wall of exhaustion. Everything was such a huge, huge effort.

My family encouraged me as far as possible to do a little more each day. If one day I managed to walk nine steps, then next day it had to be ten, or twelve – but never on any account less than nine. I suppose I invited frustration by still hoping against hope that something big and dramatic would happen to make me suddenly right again. I was still trying to reject the fact that there were no short cuts to recovery.

Mum and Dad took me to a horse trial at Knowlton Park that autumn, in October. I yearned for a great light to flash, some magic wand to wave, to make me again a competitor rather than a spectator. But nothing happened. All I could register were the people I knew I might have beaten, while there I was unable to walk, let alone ride. I was just useless.

Yet another problem was my appearance. I had put on an extra third of my original body weight and was dreadfully bloated, due to the fact that my brain was making too much body fluid instead of dissipating it in energy. To add insult to injury, some people were openly making derogatory remarks about my size.

'You have put on weight, haven't you?' was the most common sort of remark I least liked to hear.

My accident had been reported in the newspapers, and one or two of the more popular journals had used some quite embarrassing headlines. I find them funny now, but at the time I was of course unaware of them. I was known to the tabloids as the Coma Girl. 'Horsey Noises Wake Coma Girl' is one example that amuses me. Harold Judd, our old swimming instructor, who had a night job at the *Sunday Express* at the time, had read about my accident and when my parents telephoned to ask if he could help in any way, he was only too willing.

It was two days after I had stood up in my bedroom. The family had been talking about little else. It was clear to them that everything that could possibly be done should be done to improve my mobility. My father took the view that moving in water would be helpful since water would support my weight. When he told me that he wanted me to exercise in the swimming pool, my first reaction was one of amazement. If I could not walk, how could I swim? Then I thought of Mr Judd. Perhaps he could get me back to normal. I would feel safe with him. I turned to my parents and told them that I would try the pool if they could persuade Mr Judd to help me, not knowing that that was exactly what Mum and Dad had in mind.

Harold Judd (swimming teacher)

I didn't know what to think at all, when I saw
Georgina Colthurst for that first time in six years.

I'd had the pleasure of teaching her and all her brothers to swim – front and back crawl, and the breast stroke – when each was no more than three or four. I thought I'd done as much as I could for Georgina when I heard that at ten she'd started winning race after race at her school near Wheatlands, their house in Kent where I used to teach them in the garden pool.

So when her father phoned at the end of the summer of 1977 to say she needed therapy following her accident, though I hadn't seen the family for several years, I expected more or less the same Georgina. She'd been a typically athletic young English girl: tall for her age, beautifully fit, with merry hazel eyes and long, very dark hair. She'd liked to sit and listen to my swimming stories, and especially about the second year I won the one-mile sea race between the Brighton piers. It was just after the war, and on that occasion I'd managed to climb the ladder to the top to welcome the chap who came second from up there.

But I didn't recognise Georgina when I arrived at the familiar house. From her face to her feet she was puffed up and bloated, but with no muscle. She seemed to be all ballooning skin, and yet still her bones stood out. The long, shiny brown hair had been cut to stubble. Her left arm was bent unnaturally across her, and that first afternoon she had to be half-carried down to the same pool where I'd taught them all.

So we began, forty-five minutes daily at the start,

and the whole family came in too, encouraging and helping. First I had her walking in the shallow end, with me backing in front of her, holding her hands. From there, we went on to the breast stroke arm movements, especially for her left arm, pushing it with her right. And then we went on to the leg movements, all in the shallow end.

She was always hustling and bustling to get on faster, but when we started her pushing off the side to glide, she went under and I had to pull her gasping to the surface. So from then on I insisted she wore water wings and a lifebuoy ring until she could float again. She fought every inch because she said it made her feel stupid, but I got my way.

Next we started her off using fins, for more resistance from the water in order to build up her thighs.

It was very strange, all of it, re-teaching someone you'd known years before, whom you'd taken through the exact things you were now doing again. It was as though I'd never taught her at all. She was learning everything, right from the start. It was forced home to me what a terrible price a head injury can make a person pay. Everything she'd learned over the years as an infant and as a little girl, and then into teenage, she was having to learn again, but now without the coordination that had been so natural. She was having to make her limbs do things they didn't want to do, not as an athlete pushing past pain barriers to get higher performance, but simply getting her body to function at all.

It was the same with her voice. The Georgina I'd known had had a light, pleasant, lilting voice, which was a pleasure to hear. But now it was slurred, high and shrill, and the words were often garbled, coming in the wrong order.

But the determination was the same. It's hard to describe how much effort and will she put into her swimming that autumn. Nothing was ever satisfactory to her, or to her family. They always wanted not that little bit more, but usually an impossibly big bit more. So often I felt sorry for her as she dragged herself back to the house each day, obviously tired out, but in a few minutes she'd be dried and changed and back in the playroom, practising her writing or pedalling the exercise bike until her head hung with exhaustion, sweat running down her face and arms.

By the end of October she was back to diving off the springboard, and swimming back and front crawl as well as breast stroke, and she had tried the butterfly. True, she couldn't control her in-water breathing properly because the muscles you need for that were still uncoordinated with her brain. So she shipped and choked out a lot of water, and her strokes were pretty untidy – but what an achievement, from being in a deep coma three months before!

As the weeks and then months went by, the weather became cooler and I thought they would have to make some other arrangements with an indoor pool somewhere, but no. They produced a great plastic canopy and a big hot-air blower and turned the pool from an outdoor facility to an indoor one, and every day the swimming went on, exercise after exercise. With first frost, and then later with snow on the paths, they went down to get into the water.

We had also started work in the playroom to get the fingers moving. I asked Georgina to crumple newspaper with both hands and to squeeze a tennis ball. I used to think these things up on the daily and then weekly drives from Tonbridge, where I lived. I've always been a believer in yoga, and we had Georgina in due course in half-lotus, and stretching her spine (lying on her stomach and pushing up with her hands), and doing foot rotations as well.

About this time, too, she had started regular visits to the Queen Elizabeth Military Hospital in Woolwich, to do physiotherapy, and I had to be careful not to suggest anything that might be cutting across work she was doing there. I was still concerned at the tiredness of her, because she just did not seem able to tell herself to stop. The determination to work her body and mind back to normal was pushing her to limits I would not have thought possible, but of course the improvements were just as encouraging. She had begun to walk properly and use her hands and arms more or less normally, and her voice had over the months come down in pitch, and she was formulating what she wanted to say better and better. And then she started to go back to school, and almost from the time she'd returned to Wheatlands in the first place, she'd been back on her ponies and horses.

It all seemed to be working better and better as 1977 came to an end, and as I began my last visits to the Kent house, her progression had got as far as playing table-tennis with her injured left hand.

I've always been interested in everything physical. I've taken part in representative swimming and instruction, and judo (which I also taught the Colthurst children), and weight-training and so on, and over the years I've seen many remarkable feats. But Georgina's self-imposed recovery ranks among the most praiseworthy, and I was flattered and touched when at my very last visit I was told that, when she first heard swimming was recommended, she'd said she would only take part if 'my Mr Judd came to do it'.

I liked that, very much.

Corinne Barnett (ballet teacher)

Georgina Colthurst first attended my ballet classes at the age of five at a delightful little school in Surrey, near my home, and it is through young ones such as her that I have such happy memories of teaching dancing.

For I must confess, this appealing small girl with her dark hair and hazel/green eyes won my heart immediately. She tackled everything with such enthusiasm, a quality I particularly admire. With me she passed four ballet examinations, gaining Highly

Commended or Commended on each occasion, and she also took part in many school productions, both acting and dancing. I remember her especially in a Skater's Ballet – I believe she could already perform creditably on ice skates, even then – looking utterly captivating.

Of course I very soon realised that Georgina's first love was riding – how could one not! – and although I didn't see her on horseback, I'd heard she was an extremely promising young rider with a brilliant future ahead of her.

Then we lost touch for a few years when she moved on to St Michael's School at Oxted, near her home, before suddenly Fate stepped in and our paths crossed again. One September afternoon in Jubilee Year, there was a knock on our door. It was Sir Richard Colthurst, to tell me of Georgina's accident. He explained she had been unconscious for seven weeks, that her speech was impaired, and that she was having to learn to walk again. He was particularly concerned that her general coordination had suffered, and he put it to me that with the constant requirement in ballet for balance, spring and rhythmic movement, perhaps a return to dance would be of benefit.

I agreed, absolutely.

And so began our lessons together. On my first visit to their home, hearing the slurred speech and seeing her stumbling clumsiness, my heart went out to her. It seemed dreadfully unfair.

We decided that exercises at the *barre* would be the

best starting point. The radiator and the window sill in the playroom served as our *barre*, and to a tape recorder we began the slow and painful progress of strengthening the muscles to regain her mobility and poise as I had known it.

Visiting her home once or twice a week, I was soon astonished to see her progress. The old determination and enthusiasm were not only there still: if anything, they were present in even greater abundance.

She was naturally highly frustrated at first, limping about with her body simply refusing to do what she required of it. Of course, coordination was our greatest problem. From the beginning she was walking in a sort of rolling gait with little control even in that most basic of movements. I was so concerned, and I seriously wondered if anything would really be possible. But her courage and determination never ceased to amaze me. I knew she was in pain for much of the time, but she remained undeterred and forced herself through every exercise, however tough, with her sense of humour shining through.

We gradually evolved specialised exercises for her, working through from the fingers to the arms, trunk, legs, feet and finally to the toes, and little by little we began coordinating the simplest moves, first by themselves, and then one following another.

She had particular problems with her left arm; it was part-bent at the elbow, and she could not extend it fully during our earlier lessons. But then her visits to various physiotherapists began to complement our own work and gradually flexion and extension came back. From there, as Georgina reminded me, it was just like old times, working through from *barre* to *port de bras*, *adage*, and steps of elevation.

Early in the new year her ability to spring began to return, albeit very slowly. Here, her ankle joints were extremely stiff and at first that rather defeated me, but then I had a brainwave. I thought tap-dancing would give the suppleness we needed, and this, an entirely new venture for Georgina, helped loosen not only her ankles, but her knees also.

That eight-month period, until April in the year following the accident, was a time of tremendous challenge for both of us, and I found it so rewarding and exciting to watch her returning coordination and ease of movement.

She had continued to ride during this time, too, and in March – almost unbelievably, for me – she actually began horse trialling again.

My eventual ambition for Georgina was for her to dance a perfect Viennese waltz, for that would demand everything of her found-again skills. It requires general balance, movement and spring both in, and from, the feet, with forward drive from the legs in each one-beat, and coordination in the *chassés* of the two- and three-beats, and also contra-body movements – the hips rotating in the opposite direction to the shoulders – in the reverse turns, as well as, naturally, simple endurance.

Late that spring we practised, practised, practised

and practised, and on our final afternoon we swept triumphantly round and round and round the playroom again and again and again . . .

I have often wondered whether I would have responded to my situation in the same way if I had come from a different background. Of course I had inherited my family's tenacity, and everybody reacts differently according to their individual circumstances. I am also fortunate in that my family is very supportive. Someone less determined and less protected might have found recovery more difficult, but basically my problems were those of anybody who suffers a head injury and I hope that my experiences may help others, no matter what their circumstances, who are either victims of accidents or who have to look after victims.

I want to stress that nothing need be impossible for those who face problems, of whatever sort. Any major illness or injury should be approached in as positive a frame of mind as possible. Difficult as it sometimes is, we should never despair, and we should also keep our minds open to different methods of recovery. Assuming that one has the best medical attention, an ancillary therapy that suits an individual should be used. There is no substitute for loving care if it is available. Some people will benefit from prayer and religious support, others from alternative medicine. In my case we tried physiotherapy, healing, osteopathy, cranial osteopathy, chiropractic, ballet, sport – in fact whatever was available to us.

Some people imagine that all this was possible because of

my background. I feel very proud to be part of such a loving family, and fortunate to have a swimming pool and ponies at home. But I did not get well because my parents could afford to pay for my treatment. People assume that all my hospital care was under private medicine. In fact, it was mostly the reverse. The weeks of wonderful Brook treatment (in a crumbling, redundant Victorian pile heroically kept functioning) and further months of physiotherapy at the Queen Elizabeth Military Hospital, were all under the National Health Service. For that, my family and I are deeply grateful. Only my eight days at St Thomas's Hospital were funded from the private sector.

Despite his many commitments, my father still, somehow, made time to put me first. For instance, when I was being taught to ride again near Aldershot, he would help me load up in Kent at dawn; then, in his City suit, he would drive the horse-box seventy miles or so into Hampshire, catch a train to London, put in his day there and then train back to Hampshire before driving me back to Kent to assist in settling the horses for the night. That made a very long day for him, and he did this a couple of times a week for two months.

My mother was hardly ever off duty where I was concerned and my brothers were also very caring although all extremely busy. When I returned home they came to see me whenever they could.

I certainly had facilities close to hand, and it would have been ridiculous not to use them, but they would have been quite valueless without the family's support. I know, however, that if it had been unforthcoming, there would have been other ways of recovery open to me. For example,

Riding for the Disabled is a wonderful organisation with groups throughout the country. Their President is the Princess Royal and their headquarters are at the National Equestrian Centre at Stoneleigh in Warwickshire. I know that they would have helped me had I needed their help.

In fact if I did not believe that my experience was fairly typical and that it could help and encourage others who face head injuries or similar problems, I would not be writing this book. I would simply shrug my shoulders and get on with my life. Looking back now at my situation then, I realise that I might have died. Perhaps that would have been better than becoming a cabbage, which was one possibility, for the quality of life available to me was most uncertain. I might have needed assistance forever. In fact a complete recovery was doubtful.

In my case I now believe that my recovery, although aided enormously by others, was in the last analysis down to me. I want to make this point very strongly to anyone unfortunate enough to suffer injury. You have to work at getting better, believe in the possibility and never give up hope.

Everything was an effort and I had to adjust to things that other people did automatically. I am not referring to major things such as eating and dressing, but such minor things as switching on a light. Becoming tired so quickly made me annoyed but I gradually accepted that getting angry about it not only did not help; it made me even more tired.

The first part of August went by like that, and then something else quite new and alien to me came about. As I began to do the smallest things, I found myself unsure, even a bit frightened, in case I could not repeat the achievement. I did not want progress to stop. Progress was the one thing I lived for. But having established a sort of platform, being able to do something, I sometimes hardly dared to do it again in case I failed. There were many instances of this – as there had to be, when I was really no more than a toddler again, learning to walk, talk, think, remember, reason and so on.

The one skill I wanted to regain more than any other was riding and I knew I should begin by simply tacking up a pony. Looking back, I think that the most routine of operations had been preying on my subconscious.

As I had been with horses almost daily for twelve years, often riding several a day, tacking up was second nature to me, an automatic process, no more demanding than brushing my teeth or making a bed. Or rather, it had been so.

Usually the horses would cooperate, even being pleased to have bridle and saddle put on. Sometimes they could be awkward and sometimes downright difficult, and I've had hundreds of bumps and bruises to prove it. All depends on their perception of the rider.

Experts differ widely as to what intelligence is possessed by a horse. Some claim it is a creature of habit and instinct only. Others maintain that its perceptiveness reveals intelligence in advance of our own, though not the same sort of intelligence.

Certainly a horse will answer almost invisible and often unconscious signs from humans. However good an actor you are, your horse will know if you are apprehensive or confident, or anything else, the second you step into view, and very often if he cannot actually see you or (as you may think) even hear or sense you. I am certain that at the Tidworth Final Selection Trial before my accident, Folly knew what was at stake. There is a saying that your feelings go down the reins.

So, to one late August afternoon that year. My parents and two of my brothers were at home. It was 2.30 pm and oppressively hot. Everything was quiet in the house as I rose from my after-lunch rest with one thought in my head, seemingly out of nowhere. I was going to tack up Tiny.

I tried to be as quiet as a mouse because I wanted to surprise everybody. I blundered off the bed and over to the wardrobe, where I fumbled for a pair of jeans and a blouse. I had to stay on the floor to slide my legs into the jeans and as usual I had to concentrate to make my fingers coordinate to put on my shoes. The effort almost finished me off before I started.

After a couple of minutes' rest on the floor, trying to control the shaking as I fumbled a belt round the bundled clothes at my waist, I moved off, out to the landing, and downstairs, holding the special banister.

I managed to get the saddle down from the stand and then lifted the bridle from its peg, astonished at their weight. They made my shuffling walk even harder, but I put one foot in front of the other, concentrating on each step and keeping my balance, heading into the sun for the boxes.

I got there and put the saddle on the door and the bridle on the hook. I was dripping with sweat after doing so little. Ears pricked, Tiny sidled over and nuzzled my pocket in the hope of a mint. That had the effect of bringing his head down and I tried to put the bridle on him but my arms would not work. Reins over head, right arm around head, bit into mouth from left hand: that was the drill but it did not work. I simply could not coordinate and I seemed to be getting tangled up with his mane.

He watched me intently as I tried again. What followed would be hilarious as a speeded-up film. I got the reins over on his neck, and the headband on his poll after great effort, along the way catching it over one ear. I had constantly to pause to muster my forces again, first controlling my breathing and then working out what to do first before deciding how to do it. My left hand was useless of course and I fumbled with my right hand in the proper direction with the correct thing in it – bit or rein or browband or whatever, but I was all over the place. My hands did not seem to work with my shifting feet.

Throughout, Tiny stood like a statue, except for pushing his head into the bridle for me, almost willing me to succeed. He never once moved away, never once evaded my bungling and groping.

Thinking out what to do and then in what order to do it was as tiring as actually doing it. I was so delighted when I managed somehow to succeed with the bridle, enabling me to concentrate on the saddle. I leaned over the saddle. Since my left hand could not go under the pommel to take the weight, I had to manage only with my right hand, which I finally got under the cantle. I tried a dozen times to push the saddle up on Tiny's back. When eventually I managed it, it was not in the proper position.

Tiny stood still like stone as I pushed and pulled. I was

scared stiff of letting go in case the saddle fell off him. I did not think I could get it up there a second time.

Next came the part where he always fooled about. I dropped the girth three or four times before I managed to do up one buckle, but the one next to it was easier. I wondered if Tiny would try to bite in his usual playful way. I drew the strap under his belly and, for a wonder, the buckles on the other side did up fairly easily.

Once more he stood, patient and rock steady. Not even a nip. Nothing.

I leant back in triumph against the wall. I do not think I have ever in my life felt so exhausted. I had done it. I had tacked him up alone, without any help from anyone. I looked down at my watch. I remember that it was twenty-eight minutes past three.

I fumbled the door back and shuffled out ahead of Tiny, keeping my feet out of the way as he moved beside me into the sunshine. This will show everyone, I thought to myself.

We edged over to the dwarf wall by the feed-room. Using his withers, I hauled myself up to stand on top of the foot-high wall. My useless left hand would not hold the stirrup, so I rested my left arm on the saddle and, twisting my skeletal waist, with my right hand I pushed the iron over my left foot.

I was up again, and as a result of my own efforts.

For me, returning to riding meant advancing on all fronts. With hindsight, that may have been asking too much, but I suppose that was better than not trying at all. Meanwhile, Mr Neil-Dwyer's contacts and influence, and the willingness of the Army to help, opened the doors of the Queen

Elizabeth Military Hospital gymnasium at Woolwich, and so I started physiotherapy there in early September, amid the injured, some of them dreadfully, from Northern Ireland and elsewhere.

Major Charles Jones RAMC *(senior physiotherapist)*

I remember Georgina Colthurst's time at the Queen Elizabeth as a highlight in thirty years of planning, supervising and administering physiotherapy all over the world.

With her enormous enthusiasm and infectious good humour, she lightened everyone's day, be he crippled paratrooper from Belfast or arthritic general in retirement, and from the Millwall footballers to Maisie in our telephone exchange.

She came to us at a time of 'firsts' for the Queen Elizabeth. It first opened in 1977, the year of her accident, with the first purpose-built Physiotherapy Department in a British Military Hospital, which, incidentally, it had been my privilege to create from first concept to first patient.

And indeed, Georgina was our first civilian patient, resulting from the Army's keenness to cooperate and integrate with the civil community in general, with the RAMC reinforcing local National Health Service facilities in particular.

She was a happy handful, for sure. Her injuries impeded her concentration on essentially repetitive work, but when we enlisted Maggie Nicholls, our very youngest trainee therapist, the rapport – peals and shrieks of laughter, pop songs on their exercise-mat tape-players, and even their identical clothes (it was the time of Mark Phillips-style flat caps and hacking jackets) – helped mould an ideal work relationship. (Rod Stewart's 'We Are Sailing' will stay in my memory into the next world.)

Her difficulties – her left side was part-paralysed, from face to foot – meant development therapy. From birth, a baby first rolls, then lifts its head, then crawls, kneels, and stands with, and then without, support. Then it walks, and finally runs. With Georgina, we established a starting point in this progression, and from there began helping her re-learn her abilities, from that first morning when her father brought her limping in for the thrice-weekly sessions, with her short-cropped hair peeping under the tweed cap, smiling nervously but so keen to start.

She did progress, though that very enthusiasm did actually handicap her early on. Her exercise schedule was tiring, but she would push herself to exhaustion, sweating and trembling on the mats despite Maggie's entreaties to ease off.

And clearly, she was working even harder at home in between times, and not always at the right exercises. Our strategy for the spasticity of her left arm, which at the beginning hung and flapped out of control, was to allow the joints of shoulder, arm, wrist and hand passively to regain their proper positions – by establishing the limb in its correct mode, and leaving it to adapt to that – and thence their normal functions. But certain of the supplementary exercises she so eagerly practised away from us were actively working muscle in those areas, which was the exact reverse requirement at that point.

But on we went: first mat work – 'bridging' (on the back, then up into support on hands and feet) and so on – and gradually to weight bearing properly, and then to the benches, working and strengthening all the muscles down that left side, throughout the range of each.

The visits dropped back to twice a week as planned, and in the second month to once weekly, while the therapy at her home built up with her swimming-pool exercises, and she went back to ballet classes with our approval – the re-learning of overall control, and balance and spring, would mean interaction of her muscle groups, and exactly what she required.

When Maggie had her really hurtling round the badminton courts, we felt she could progress best away from the Queen Elizabeth. It's always difficult to decide when that moment comes for a patient, and certainly we knew we'd miss her bouncing in and out of rooms and corridors and cubicles, chattering with anyone and everyone about families and Ireland and horses, and above all the yells and yells of laughter – and that included Maggie, and her young Warrant Officer supervisor Don Bartlett, and

9a My first attempt at writing on my return home from hospital in July 1977.

9b A birthday card to my mother, 7 August 1977.

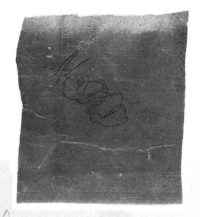

28 8 77.   P 8 1

Dear Nan.

I am very thirsty this...

letter to you to thank you for lunch, thank
you again for lunch plenty of drink I hope I
will have a swim after that bicycle and a swim
hope, I will drink the swimming pool I
will ride Tony on the Ghost after
lunch and Snoopy at home because he bits
that is rolling off. Am I writing better
and I hope the swim warms me up.
Charles is reading Hemingway A Farewell To
Arms well—that his all.

Lots of Love from
Georgina, xx xxxoo

10 A letter to Nan, my mother's
old nanny, at the end of August
1977. (Note the constant references
to thirst!)

11a The inevitable horse drawn by me in August 1977.

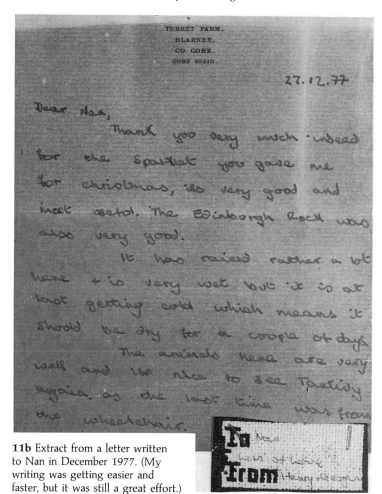

TURRET FARM,
BLARNEY,
CO. CORK.
CORK 85210.

27.12.77

Dear Nan,

Thank you very much indeed for the spotlet you gave me for christmas, its very good and most useful. The Edinborgh Rock was also very good.

It has rained rather a lot here + is very wet but it is at last getting cold which means it should be dry for a couple of days. The animals here are very well and its nice to see Tautivy again, as the last time was from the wheelchair.

11b Extract from a letter written to Nan in December 1977. (My writing was getting easier and faster, but it was still a great effort.)

To Nan
lots of love
From Henry

12a On the farm in Ireland before the accident, 1976.

12b My first passport photo after the accident. It took a long time for my hair to regain its strength.

13a On Folks Folly at the Tidworth Three-Day Event Junior Trial, 1977, shortly before the accident.

13b On Folks Folly a year later at the Tidworth Three-Day Event Junior Trial. I had put on weight after the accident and had very little balance in the saddle, so poor Folly was obliged to compensate.

14a On Tullig at the Windsor Horse Show, 1979. The lefthand side of my face had not fully recovered after the accident.

14b On Wily Woodpecker, representing Great Britain at Boekelo, 1983.

15a Eventing is a family affair — with my parents in front of the horse box, 1986.

15b Henry's wedding to Sophie, 1983. Back row, left to right: James, Charles, my father, my mother, Henry, Sophie (née Harvey-Bathurst), members of Sophie's family. I am at the lefthand end of the front row.

16 Cross-country schooling at Milton Keynes Equestrian Centre
on Limerick Lear, April 1990.

indeed the whole shifting population of battlefield and training and sporting injuries which made up our busy life at the Queen Elizabeth.

At her final assessment, as we chatted and I took notes, I couldn't help remembering her first day and the transformation from the shuffling, apprehensive hemiplegic to this sparkling young lady who couldn't wait to get to grips again with life.

But here, I have to register one reservation, and that was over her determination to return to equestrian sport.

Riding for the Disabled is an established therapeutic institution, well supported by the medical profession, and certainly by myself. But, and generally speaking here, whether riding is right for the head-injured, where one knock could result in more serious and lasting damage, I am not sure.

However, Georgina and her parents were adamant that not only riding, but riding at international level, was her normal life. And, after carefully weighing up all the factors, they (and most of all, Georgina) had decided she should go ahead. That she has done so must be due in large part to phenomenal ability as well as extraordinary application by herself, and those around her. It is far from certain that this course would succeed with everyone in such a situation, or indeed that it would even be right.

Having said that, the great diversity of physical, mental and spiritual help afforded Georgina, coupled with her own drive and determination, will give heart to countless other head-injured patients and their families. In facing the long and difficult road back to recovery and reintegration, they now have an example in a particularly fine young woman.

Mr Neil-Dwyer thought that I would derive more stimulus, as well as receive the best attention, in the excellent atmosphere of the Queen Elizabeth Military Hospital among seriously injured people. Needless to say, their equipment was the most sophisticated and up-to-date. There was an enormous gym with every conceivable apparatus and a pool for aquatherapy. Fortunately, it was Army policy to afford spare capacity to the community at large, and I was therefore admitted as their first civilian patient. The hospital not only caters for injured in-patients but provides fitness training for Army sportsmen, specifically at the time for rugger players. A number of the physiotherapists in fact were members of rugger teams.

Mum and Dad drove me to Woolwich for my assessment interview and I managed somehow to walk into the hospital on my own two feet. It had only been officially opened weeks before by the Queen Mother.

My visit, however, started with a slight hitch. The Army, usually so well organised, did not expect a head-injured patient to arrive on foot. They were looking out for somebody in a wheelchair. We were shown into a small waiting-room where we sat and sat until finally Dad asked a Warrant Officer if anyone could help. This brought immediate action and, after some embarrassed apologies, we started on a series of interviews and examinations, beginning with the senior medical officer, Colonel Robinson, and then the officer in charge of physiotherapy, Captain (later Major) Charles Jones.

It was decided that since I was receiving positive help at home, so that for example I did not need the hospital's swimming pool, I could be treated at the Queen Elizabeth as a day patient, and initially I attended three mornings a week.

At all times there was an amazingly happy atmosphere, which was astonishing in a place where there were so many injured. I got on really well with Maggie Nicholls and Don Bartlett, my two special contacts, who with Chas, as Captain Jones was known, were responsible for a great deal of laughter.

There were plenty of women physios but, in my section at least, I was for a time the only female patient. This in no way bothered anyone, least of all me, because the atmosphere was so friendly and it was not much different from having three brothers at home. What was unusual was that I was in the company both of a large number of fit, dedicated and highly disciplined young men and also of injured and handicapped patients.

Throughout there was the relentless, positive cheerfulness. From the first instant I never felt I was being pitied or patronised, or regarded as an oddity for special treatment. I was a perfectly normal person, among other perfectly normal people. That we had little temporary problems was unremarkable. Soldiers flown in from Northern Ireland with legs and arms blown off, or arriving from Belize or

Hong Kong after diseases in the jungles or wounds from operational training, were treated kindly and sensibly.

At the Queen Elizabeth, problems were facts of life, to be tackled and overcome without delay. Indeed, as time went by I myself was encouraged to go and cheer up new arrivals – I remember particularly two severely burned soldiers and a WRAC girl – in the physiotherapy ward. I was put in charge of the ward temporarily on one occasion and did not make too great a mess of things!

My uneven gait and my flapping arm were absolutely normal there. Maggie used to help my concentration and memory by shooting sudden questions at me:

'What time did you get up?'

'0600 hours!' I would reply in Army fashion.

'Where are your brothers today?'

'James is at St Thomas's. Charles is in the City somewhere. Henry – I don't know!'

'Think!'

'Got it! He's gone to Newmarket.'

'What did you have for breakfast?'

'Cereal, toast and orange juice.'

We also worked on voluntary movement, using neighbouring muscles to work my weaker ones – a technique called 'overflow'.

Another lasting memory of that time is thirst. On the first day, at our mid-morning break, I drank a whole pint of milk and a whole pint of squash, one straight after the other. I was often quite hungry too, after all the exercise, and Maggie had to restrict my intake, although she often rewarded me with a drink or a chocolate bar from the little WRVS shop after I had completed a series of exercises.

Slowly, visit by visit, we could see and I could feel the improvement. It was like getting back to first principles, infant skills, and building from there – in fact just as to all intents and purposes, I was learning to ride from scratch again.

My particular concern was still my left arm. It was not straight and I did so want it to be, in order to conform with the world outside.

I know that my urgent frustration and anxiety to improve quickly were wearing on Maggie and I owe much to her patience and good humour. Nothing was ever too much trouble, her tolerance was wonderful, and we always had the safety valve of jokes and laughter.

All activities overlapped. As I started to master one set of exercises, but before I had quite done so, we would start another. I was encouraged to try my hand at badminton and Maggie and I were kindly invited to play doubles with two friendly Millwall footballers, who were having treatment at the same time.

I gradually reduced my visits until I was only going to the Queen Elizabeth once a week, and in due course Colonel Robinson and Charles Jones decided that I had progressed as far as I could with them and that improvement should be sustained from there by my activities at home.

I was deeply sorry to clamber back into the car on my last day and I have tried hard to keep in touch with the truly remarkable people there.

A great healing hospital like the Queen Elizabeth of course concentrates on basic mobility. Intricate movements sometimes need special attention. For example I needed to gain flexibility in my hands and I resorted to a trick of Harold Judd's, namely crumpling up newspapers to strengthen my fingers.

With one exception, there were no great landmarks after the Queen Elizabeth until the following spring. I had taken to using my left hand rather than the more natural right for as many things as possible – such as eating or brushing my hair – in order to help get the left side more mobile. I think it helped to loosen the wrist and fingers, although the concentration required was still a problem. I used my right hand, however, to write my Christmas cards that year. My writing was still bad but just about legible.

The exceptional landmark was an affiliated jumping competition, on Folly, in December. I should not dwell on it really because he was eligible for more advanced classes, but after a clear round John Smart, who had been teaching me, turned to Dad and said: 'Just look at her face! That says it all.' I was indeed delighted. This was my first positive result since my accident.

Looking at the schedules for the following spring, I worked out a hopeful programme that included possible selection for the Junior European Three-Day Event Trials at Tidworth in May. This may have been ambitious but it gave me hope and a target to aim for. I decided that a small dressage competition at Coakham in January would make a good start. It did not worry me that Coakham was where I had had my fall. It was local, I did not have to worry about travelling and it was nothing spectacular. It would be a pleasant little country meeting.

In early September I had a vivid dream that I could swim again as I had been able to before the accident. The following day, I had a long session in the pool with Mr Judd. I had become more and more impatient with the unspeakable children's water-wings and the lifebuoy he made me wear. I truly hated those childhood reminders. They were visible evidence that I was really the same now as I had been when I first used them at the age of four in our 1965 lessons. The stupid things also impeded my arm movements and set up resistance to forward motion. I was certain I could swim without them along the surface, as I had once been able.

I was at the poolside and waiting for Mr Judd as he came smiling down the path that afternoon. I remember every word we said then.

'Hello, Georgina! How are you feeling today? Ready for the swim?'

'Yes,' I said. 'Would you let me swim today without the armbands and the ring? Just once, please?'

Mr Judd was never less than polite. He hesitated.

'Look, let me try just one width. Just one. It's only twenty feet. Across the shallow end, not the deep end. You come in with me and stand in the middle. So, if I do sink, you'll only have at most ten feet to go to pull me up.' I had worked it all out. 'Please, Mr Judd.'

When he had positioned himself halfway across, I bent at the knees and launched myself at the other side.

It cannot have been beautiful to watch. I was wallowing along in a wall of spray with my arms flailing and my legs thrashing in a parody of my dream's speed-swimming, but I was going forward without the rings, and sure enough one hand finally slapped on the far side surround. I had done it. This was another small victory.

Tomorrow I was going to have another go. I was determined this time to swim a length. I knew that everyone would object but I already had my tactics worked out. Tomorrow was Saturday, so James and Henry would be there, and Mum and Dad of course. If I started at the deep end, and as I had already proved by swimming a width that I could get approximately half a length, I would be in the shallow end if I started to tire. So one of the boys could stay about half way, with perhaps someone else between him and the deep end, just in case.

And that was how we did it. Afterwards I took the wings back to the house for good.

After my first attempt to tack up and mount Tiny alone I was naturally apprehensive about doing the same thing properly a second time, but I knew that progress must be maintained. I was worried, however, not only about my strength, but about whether I could remember what to do and in what order. I need not have worried because in the event I managed the whole thing in half the time. It is amazing how quickly one can pick up or improve on skills, far more readily than seemed possible at the outset. It is a matter of application and continuity. Talent of course comes into it but more important than great talent is commitment – and that I certainly had.

Before that hot afternoon when I had sweated to tack Tiny up, I had been put up on him in the paddock, as I have said, but what worried me from the start was that I had so dreadfully little balance and that I swayed like a tree in a gale. In order to ride well, you have to be as instinctively balanced, and as fit and supple, as your mounts. Back on

Tiny in the paddock, with my old jeans bundled around my bony waist and legs, I set about recovering my riding form. Coordination and balance were the problems but we pressed on, and after two weeks of persistent effort I managed to get Tiny up to a trot and still stay aboard.

Then one morning I decided to risk something a little more ambitious. I asked him to canter. It was a marvellous feeling to be out of the eternal walk and trot.

Then I became more adventurous still and practised the advanced dressage movements I had taught him – including the Lippizaner tricks – in previous years.

From that time I felt that jumping was just around the corner.

I knew that a full and rewarding existence for me must entail riding to the limits of my ability, but I had to start again at a very basic level. Dad reconstructed some of the small twig-and-branch jumps in between trees in the field at the bottom of our garden, and I started jumping them with Tiny. Minnie and Snoopy were too powerful and would have jumped too big for me.

The inevitable of course happened. Tiny always tended to cat-jump. In other words, he would approach a fence and slow down almost to a stop before jumping it. On one occasion, in the first week of resuming the baby jumping, his rider rolled off him, unable to keep her balance during one of his jerky jumps!

Jolted but unhurt, I pushed myself upright as Dad hurried over, and I blurted out the only thing in my head. 'Don't – don't tell Mum. Please!'

'Are you all right?' he said anxiously.

'Of course I am,' I almost shouted, 'but please don't tell Mum. She'll stop me altogether if she finds out. Please don't. You won't, will you? Please!'

He shook his head. 'Well, let's see if you can do it properly,' he said. 'Try the same fence again.'

I scrambled back up on Tiny, desperate to get this next jump in, not just properly but perfectly. I took him round to approach the same little fence, and I whispered words to convey exactly what was at stake if he failed me now of all times. Tiny did his job. I turned and looked back. I was pleased to see Dad clapping his hands.

'You won't tell Mum, will you?' I begged as I dismounted.

'No,' he smiled gravely. 'I won't.'

I think actually she had seen the whole thing from a bedroom window. At any rate, that very day she suggested that I resume riding instruction and thought that Deirdre Robinson, who had helped me through Pony Club exams, was the right person to get me going again.

When I started riding Minnie again Dad used to walk around the woods, then send me off and meet me at an appointed place. This gave me a feeling of independence, doing something on my own. One day, when Dad was driving behind me on the road, keeping a careful eye on me, a neighbour came out to ask me whether I realised I was being followed!

I should explain that just as famous opera singers continue to take singing lessons and successful athletes are coached, so even the best riders have specialist instruction, such as dressage. Mistakes can be seen by an independent observer from the ground which may be missed by the rider on top. In my case, although I had achieved considerable expertise, I now almost had to go back to the leading rein. It was like a sixth-former going back to nursery school, because although I knew what I wanted to do and how to do it, I could not get my body to obey my brain, however hard I tried. This was of course horribly demoralising, but the very fact that riding was again part of my routine raised my spirits. In fact returning back to normal and familiar routine is one of the best methods of rehabilitation.

I had great confidence in Deirdre, who is a marvellous and patient teacher and who had helped me towards all my early successes. From the age of eight, twice a week after school and at weekends and on holidays, I used to go to her place, which has now developed into the Fleetmead Stud. On schooldays Mum always collected me and drove me over, and I used to change in the car during the nine-mile journey. My school homework waited until I got back. I usually spent an hour or two riding on weekdays and four to six hours at weekends, when I was not competing of course. At different times Folly, Tantivy, Minnie and Witch were stabled there, and Deirdre had her own animals, ranging from unbroken youngsters to her great dressage horse Oberon.

Deirdre had been appalled at my accident, because we had been so close all those years. She had serious reservations about my returning to riding at all. She wanted to help with the therapy, but the risk involved in anything but work on the flat – which for competition meant dressage only – worried her enough for her to consult her own specialist contacts. Their opinion that I risked permanent damage, or worse, if I had another fall did nothing to reassure her.

Therefore, on my first day back she could not conceal her

anxiety as I showed her what I could do, or perhaps it is better to say what I could not do. My flapping arm and uncoordinated wobbly seat could hardly have inspired her.

In the end we compromised. Deirdre would have me back for dressage only. I hoped this meant that she would prepare me for a big competition, perhaps Tidworth in the spring, but I doubt if Deirdre, or anyone else for that matter, shared my optimism.

I had to be content with what she was willing to offer me. She was worried that I might feel her concern on my behalf and that this might affect my performance.

It is Deirdre whom I have to thank for starting me back again on the road to serious riding, but I was not satisfied merely to work on the flat. Dressage was an important stage in my return to eventing but I was determined not to forget cross-country and show-jumping. I must have become a terrible nag about this to my parents, and Mum tried in vain to prevail on Deirdre to take me a stage further. Deirdre did recommend John Smart, who had been booked to give a show-jumping clinic in her school. She mentioned me to him, and despite the risks involved, he was willing to take an interest in me, having seen me at competitions before my accident.

Deirdre and John – and I must not forget Folly in particular – did an amazing job.

John Smart (riding instructor)

The first time I saw Georgina Colthurst on a horse after her accident, she scared me to death. I suppose

I could claim not to scare too easily where horses are concerned. Having survived four Badmintons and Burghleys, and other international horse trials and show-jumping events abroad as well as at home, you do reckon to have seen a certain amount. Indeed, it was that degree of experience which led me to settle in Sussex to instruct, particularly in top-level show-jumping, helping to iron out problems that occur in any rider or horse.

It was towards the end of 1977, on a dark evening at Deirdre Robinson's Fleetmead Stud in Surrey. Deirdre, an old friend and now neighbour with a phenomenal record in competing and instruction, had phoned to say that one of her former students had left hospital after a fall, and would I help assess her? I was wondering why she was asking me, with all her vast knowledge, when she added that the student was Georgina Colthurst.

It all then fell into place. I well knew, as did most in our particular part of the horse world, that Georgina had been coached by Deirdre, and that there had been a close bond between them, right from when the youngster had been a toddler with her first ponies.

I had known of Georgina's fall and hospitalisation: it's not every day that one of our most brilliant prospects has that happen. So now she was up and about and Deirdre had been approached to start her off training again, and she wanted my opinion. Fine by me.

I was particularly looking forward to meeting

Georgina. They were unloading Folks Folly as I went over. Deirdre was off to one side with the parents, so I strolled up to Georgina to say hello and watch her tack up.

That brought the first flutter of alarm. She was hardly using her left arm or hand, and when she spoke her speech was slurred and her face looked stiff on the left side. Then when she climbed aloft, swaying, and settled somehow, I thought: there is *no* way she should be allowed near a horse.

They moved off into the school, the girl swaying in the saddle even at walk, and as I wondered how I could break to the parents what I was feeling, Lady Colthurst came across to me.

'I know she looks pretty unstable up there just now,' she said quietly, 'but she's been cantering her ponies at home and popping over little brush fences, and she's so much improved already.'

I simply didn't know how to go about venturing my opinion, so I said: 'What do the doctors say about this?'

'The specialists told her she should get back to horses as soon as possible. They said it would be the best therapy for her, and I must say it seems to be working so far.'

Georgina had reached the far end of the school, and was turning to come trotting back, rolling precariously.

I couldn't look. I murmured something about the differences between top-level competition in show-jumping and eventing and just being with horses, and perhaps Georgina might consider some sort of career in – say – judging dressage?

Just as I said that, the girl turned the horse and headed for a little fence across the track at the other side of the school. Her left arm was flailing from the shoulder and her whole body was teetering over, but she kept on trotting for the pole and I thought 'God, this is it,' and then Folly popped the jump – and they were over, the jockey rolling and sliding about, wildly off balance. How she stayed up there I'll never know.

Five months later we were together at the Tidworth Three-Day Event, for Georgina to compete on that same course where, twelve months before, she had been shortlisted for the British Team for Fontainebleau.

If I hadn't seen and been party to it all myself, I simply wouldn't have believed it.

Was my determination to return to riding foolhardy, or justified?

Well, as a family we have always followed the maxim that where there is life, there is hope, and two of Britain's foremost neurosurgeons had refused to give me a totally pessimistic prognosis, so surely I had every reason to hope for the best. In any case I believe in the extraordinary recuperative powers of the human frame; and there seems to be no limit to what willpower can achieve.

Of course there was a risk. Riding can be dangerous, but fortunately, despite my accident, I had no fears. Rather the reverse – I felt at my most confident on top of a horse. If I had had to give up riding, I would have gone through life wondering what might have been.

Not everybody approved of my return to riding. Many people blamed my parents for pushing me. In fact it was medical advice that I be put back on a safe horse. Thereafter it was I who pushed my parents.

As it happened, I did have an early fall when I went hunting in November. It was not very serious. Somebody crossed in front of me, stopping my horse, and due to my lack of balance I fell off. Only my pride was hurt, and that not much. A friend came to pick me up and managed to catch the horse.

As far as I was concerned, I was riding again. That made it a red-letter day for me. I had taken another rung up the ladder to normality. I was improving.

At that time my main disability was my left arm because I could not straighten my elbow. Although I am right-handed, I was encouraged to try to do everything possible with my left hand in an attempt to improve that arm's mobility. My neck was crooked as the result of a vertebra having been displaced. Another problem was slight double vision, which is often associated with head injuries. My sight was at its worst when I was tired. Fortunately the double vision was intermittent after a time and gradually disappeared. Curiously it never seemed to affect me when I was riding.

I have mentioned briefly my weight problem. From being a skeleton, I suddenly found myself a fat girl, despite all the exercise I was taking. It was not until after Christmas that this became a serious factor. When I tried to put on my leather riding boots to practise for the dressage competition at Coakham, in January, I found that my calves had swollen to such an extent that I could not manage it. Luckily James was at home, and after I had struggled for a quarter of an hour I called him in to help. We tried everything we knew, all the old tricks like putting French chalk or powder on the insides, but it was only after two full hours of applied power from his strong arms that we had them on. I had no idea how I would ever get them off again. The obvious solution was to have the boots altered, but in fact I wore black rubber riding boots when the day came. My main memory of the occasion is the reaction of my friends and other competitors. 'Gosh, Georgina, you've put on so much weight,' one girl said to me. 'Are you really competing?'

Well might she have asked this question because for a long time I could hardly walk, except on flat surfaces. Walking over rough ground and toiling up and down slopes was difficult. But it was the sort of question that infuriated me. I did not need anyone to point out the obvious. Even some of my friends seemed to be arrogant and tactless, as well as patronising, even if they did not mean to be unkind. They did not perhaps realise how sensitive I was.

What was I to think when I overheard someone say, 'No one ever recovers from brain damage, do they?'

In fact it made me more determined. It would take time but I would show them what I was made of. 'Are you really sure you should be doing this?' I was very sure. 'We never thought we'd see you in competition again.' Well, here I was.

I started walking Folly around the practice area. I could feel, as well as see, the steward watching me more closely than stewards usually do, and the odd spectator, as well as my fellow competitors, seemed to be intrigued by my appearance. I tried not to think of my wobbling left arm, and, bless him, Folly was popping in the odd side-shuffle or half-step to help me as I teetered, especially in canter. It could not have looked anything but odd, I suppose.

When the steward called us, we trotted to a halt dead centre in the arena, nice and still. I inclined my head and smiled and went off down the centre line and into the test.

How time flies when you are enjoying yourself, and how it drags when you are not. That ghastly test went on forever, and the only thing right about it was the sequence. I could do nothing about the useless arm and I did try very hard, but without success, to control my body's swaying, while clever Folly kept looking after my shifting weight; I could just imagine the judges' incredulous stares and their muttered observations.

I hardly dared wait for the results.

And we were pretty well bottom.

I went back to the box in my bulging jacket and uncomfortable boots and sat in the cab and cried. I cried in frustration at having tried my best and failed, and in sorrow at having let down my loyal and caring Folly so dreadfully.

After a while I just sat there, trembling, looking down at the upturned, useless hand in my lap. And then I bit my lip.

It had been only to be expected.

There would be scores, hundreds more sorrows and humiliations like this, but I would not allow them to affect me. That was a decision I took there and then.

I was just going to go on fighting back.

It took time for my weight problem to sort itself out but as I began to regain my shape I realised of course that my brain was again starting to organise itself.

John Smart started me off with Folly at all paces, gradually allowing us to jump first over little poles and then moving on to fences proper. I seem to recall it was at a spread that I had my first gentle tumble, and I shall never forget poor John's reaction. He came running across the school, his eyes filled with concern, as I sat up and looked round for my whip.

'Georgina! Are you all right?'

'No,' I chuckled as he helped me up. 'I'm stupid. I lost impulsion on the last stride.'

'You know what I mean,' he frowned anxiously. 'Have you hurt yourself? Have you hurt anything?'

'Just my pride,' I said. 'I'm going to jump it properly this time.'

It is a practice in jumping never to finish on a bad note, so we jumped two more fences without trouble and finished the lesson happily. I am sure that John realised that certain allowances would have to be made for me, at least until I could control my balance and my wretched left arm better.

We went on, ever progressing, to and past Christmas and into the New Year.

Henry Colthurst (brother)

I returned from South Africa, where I had been working for five months, less than a week before

Georgina's accident. I remember well that first sight of her in hospital and could have wept; her eyes stared vacantly at all comers, her head lolled on its pillow and her half-shaved scalp reminded me of a Mohican Indian. Apart from the initial shock, it seemed such a tragic waste for such an energetic spirit to now appear so listless.

We had no choice but to accept the situation. I had intended to leave for Florence and Rome some three weeks later in order to study for my first term at Cambridge in the autumn; after the accident I cancelled this plan and instead opted to take a concentrated course in London in order to stay close at hand.

The doctors made it fairly clear at the beginning that if Georgina were to recover, it would take a considerable time. Long after she came home she was still not her former self. I think it took considerable pluck to re-enter the social fray, but she would not go to a dance unless accompanied by James or myself. One party in particular I remember well. It was held near Winchester over a year after the accident. She had by then regained most of her figure but there were still signs of stiffness in her left elbow and a wobbliness on her feet. These were probably not obvious to an outsider but I have a critical eye. At the same party Georgina introduced me to her closest friend Sophie with whom I danced but once. I am often reminded of that particular party; Sophie is now my wife!

Nevertheless, Georgina's early recovery appears

to have been fairly miraculous. Much of the credit must go to our parents. In fact my abiding memory of the fall and its aftermath remains the amount of time and sacrifice that my parents gave from that very first day. Their mental fatigue became visible especially as the coma dragged on its long and depressing course. Mum displayed an ever brave and patient face but she could not hide her painful anxieties. Dad stubbornly refused to capitulate; his attitude was probably quite infuriating to doctors and nurses alike but Georgina has a lot to thank for his and my mother's refusal to accept defeat, often in the face of expert opinion.

They always felt there was hope, and their convictions were rewarded. They were admittedly generous with their material support – no expense was spared. It is important to understand, however, that it was not money that formed the basis of Georgina's recovery but their own emotional support. Other families in less fortunate circumstances should understand that the patient's need is one of encouragement provided primarily by massive parental and family support – not in a material context but in an emotional and mental sense.

But whatever assistance Georgina received from her parents and from professional expertise, all the help in the world would have been useless if she had not herself possessed an extraordinary will to recover. She would never have got better if at any stage her will to survive and to improve had

surrendered. Her own remarkable determination
proved vital.

Charles Colthurst (brother)

After Georgina's accident, the doctors advised
us to keep talking to her in the hope that her
subconscious would pick up something of what we
were saying. I recall telling her that Lester Piggott
had won the Derby on The Minstrel, and I
wondered if that fact would register with her when
eventually she woke up. After she moved to St
Thomas's I started working with Humberts, the
estate agents, to get some ideas for Blarney. One
night the phone rang at home. It was my father
who said that somebody wanted to talk to me. I
took the telephone and heard Georgina making
some sort of verbal noises. She was obviously
trying extremely hard to talk but she was rather
incoherent.

Soon after her return home, I remember that she
had to be lifted on to Tiny and that on one occasion
she was given a leg up and went right over the other
side! Fortunately there was no harm done.

By the time she went to the Queen Elizabeth
Military Hospital, there were definite signs of
recovery on her part. She seemed to enjoy the
different environment where she could do all sorts
of exercises. It seemed to motivate her considerably
to see the conduct of certain soldiers who had
suffered dreadful injuries, and I recall the staff

saying that every time she came, she was a little bit better than the last time.

She came to Ireland for Christmas and the journey was extremely tiring because the plane was diverted from Heathrow to Luton. In Ireland she rode a bicycle, regularly falling off due to lack of balance. She went to the top of the castle to kiss the Blarney Stone and managed it only with difficulty. She grew incredibly tired at times and had to sleep in the afternoon.

We played cards all and every evening as there was little else that she could really concentrate on. We tried Pelmanism to improve her memory. She also tried her hand at ping-pong. She was awful at first because she could not coordinate her body movements but I became quite excited when she began to hit the ball back.

Another problem was that she often felt very cold.

One day she drove Snoopy in a trap. Snoopy came back without her and a search party was sent out. She was found walking up Fords Avenue, safe and sound. Apparently she had got out of the trap to close a gate, and Snoopy had taken off on his own.

From then on I observed steady improvement each time I saw her.

I am often asked how I got by socially.

Being at a day school, almost everyone I knew outside the horse world lived in the district all around, so I had plenty of friends and fun. But after I left St Thomas's

Hospital, the situation was quite different. Getting back to horses was all very well but life generally had to be faced too: including important matters like returning to school. Although I had slowed down physically, and mentally too in some respects, I could still see things in the round. The normality for which I aimed meant that I should be out there and mixing as soon as possible, but this was not easy for me.

The first party I went to was in November, locally. Some friends were giving a dinner dance, and I went with Henry. I tried to be on my best behaviour and not to be obtrusive but I had to keep thinking of how to keep my posture and not make a fool of myself. I was concerned about what people might be thinking of me.

My concentration was poor and my mind wandered. I found it difficult to talk for more than a few seconds. I simply could not follow or remember what was being said, and I could not contribute very much to proceedings. It did not help to say nothing because people would then think that I was unwell or shy and, in kindness, would try to draw me out. All that did was reveal my problems, and out came the muddled words in part-finished sentences. That in turn led them, albeit in the nicest way, to patronise me, which only embarrassed me and made me more anxious to do things properly and frustrated that I could not do so.

My brothers' efforts were never ending. Charles always laughed a lot and kept up spirited chat and gossip whenever he was at home. He is tremendously sociable and encouraged his friends to support me. With his boundless strength and energy, and of course his medical training, James would anticipate many problems and come up with practical solutions. Henry was especially good at helping me socialise, and I am very happy that I was able to repay him a year later by introducing him to his wife Sophie, who is my best friend.

At much the same time I returned to school, although I was not as regular an attender as I would normally have been because I had to go three times a week initially to the Queen Elizabeth. I also started ballet lessons at home in the morning as an additional form of therapy, and of course I was having swimming lessons and I was riding.

Perhaps I returned to school too soon because I was nowhere near ready for the total reintegration into my former life there.

Also there was no understanding of what head injuries do, and, to be fair, one could hardly expect everyone I met everywhere to allow for my frustrated behaviour. I was still very hazy, with my concentration flagging and my thoughts drifting away from the books and the teachers, and all the efforts being made on my behalf.

But at least I was leading a very full life and this did not leave me too much time to think about myself.

Jacqueline Tennant BSC *(biology teacher)*

The news of Georgina Colthurst's riding fall had filtered through to the staff room as these things do, and I must say when I heard she was coming back to us at St Michael's just after the start of the autumn term, I very much looked forward to teaching her again.

We all have our share of problem pupils, but

Georgina had been the very reverse, blossoming through the years into a quiet and unassuming young lady whose abilities with horses and enthusiasm for the countryside fed her appetite for my subject. So I was glad I would have this tall, hazel-eyed and popular girl back in my classes before Christmas that year – before, indeed, my own departure to take up an appointment elsewhere.

The idea was to divide her attendances between the Fifth and Sixth Forms, to suit her interrupted summer term exams schedule best, which for myself would mean coaching her back to the point where she had been ready for 'O' Level Biology, just before her accident.

Georgina stood up with the rest as I went into that first class, and although the Headmistress had warned me she wouldn't be the same, I was really quite shaken. It was a Fifth Form period, but Georgina had been allowed non-uniform status as a Sixth Form pupil, and so she stood out anyway.

But the hazel eyes staring about her from the painfully anxious face, the hair cropped within an inch of her head, and her swaying as she stood were disturbing.

We were immediately to see that her persona had changed also in every way. Where she'd had a quiet, pleasant speaking voice, now she mumbled, often unintelligibly. Before, she'd been a quietly independent and self-sufficient girl, never asking for anything, always with her books and papers and pens and pencils and so on ready to hand. She would think, come to conclusions, and only ask the most pertinent of questions. Whenever Georgina's hand went up I knew always her question, and my answer, would add dimension to what I was teaching.

But now her constant babbled interruptions actually began to unsettle the others, to the extent that I truly wondered at the wisdom of her being back with us so soon after hospital discharge. Her writing, too, previously the neatest and clearest anyone could wish for, was a hopeless spidery scrawl which neither she nor anyone else could read.

At the welcome end of that first lesson, and long after the others had gathered up books and rulers and pencil boxes and trooped out to lunch, Georgina was still tottering round her desk, as she tried to fumble things into her school bag. I felt so sorry for her, but when I went to help she insisted that she was perfectly all right, that she had to do things for herself. Actually, I didn't see much more of her from then because of my impending move, and as she had started regular visits to London for treatment, her St Michael's attendance was in any case irregular . . .

Tessa Martin-Bird FBHS *(freelance instructor)*

I knew Georgina before her accident. People with talent stand out and she had caught my eye as being a talented rider when I was judging or watching Pony Club Horse Trials.

News travels fast and I heard of the accident through the horse media and also through my brother, who had been at the same preparatory school as Georgina's brothers, so we all knew the Colthurst family.

In January 1978, I was competing at a dressage competition at Coakham, Kent, giving my horses a schooling before the Horse Trials season began. I was preparing one of my horses for the test and among the other competitors also training their horses was Georgina. I must have been very drawn by her courage and bravery and it made me watch her dressage test. I could feel my inner self saying what a tragedy it was that someone so young and talented had been so badly injured as a result of a fall, but thinking more deeply that here were we – so called 'normal' riders – struggling with our problems while she, seriously handicapped on her left side, was making a good effort at riding her dressage test.

After completing her test, we got talking and Georgina asked if I would help her train towards the Pony Club Area Horse Trials and to sit various exams within the horse world. I agreed. By now I was fully aware of her disabilities. Something inside me said that I would be able to help, but of course I realised I had a great responsibility on my hands. From our brief meeting, I knew she was determined to succeed. I did of course approach Georgina's parents (as she was only seventeen) to have their approval and to know that they would take the full responsibility of her being with me.

In 1976 I had commenced training the first Blue Peter pony for the RDA (Riding for the Disabled) and had therefore become involved with disabled people. I think this was a great turning-point for me, as I know I had always felt sorry for people with disabilities and it made me realise how lucky I was to be fit and well. From my first day working with disabled riders, I was at one with all the pupils, and the joy and satisfaction it gave, and still gives, is enormous. The psychology of teaching is always fascinating. I suppose the main difference in teaching disabled riders is that things take longer – but after all, when training young horses, or inexperienced people for that matter, one must progress slowly and clearly.

Initially, Georgina's father drove both horse and her over to me for her lessons. For the first visits, she came on her faithful horse, Folly. Her objective was the Pony Club Horse Trials and her aims always being high, she wanted to qualify for the Championships at the end of the season.

We developed a good rapport from the moment she came into the riding school and the bond to work together as a team just grew. The success rate was rapid due to her determination. She never complained, neither did she mention how unlucky she was. She had the true ingredients of what a teacher wishes to find in a pupil. She was dedicated. She wanted to work and improve with it.

Her left side was her great problem. It was fascinating to watch her ride. You were drawn to watch her because there was so much that was right in what she did, and so much obvious enjoyment for both horse and rider; yet you were also confronted with a whole heap of problems. The left arm and hand were far from coordinated and gave a very jerky appearance, but the amazing thing was that they worked in a rhythm with the horse's movement. The left leg was also a problem. This had a habit of wandering and becoming shorter, which therefore made it difficult for Georgina to keep the foot in the stirrup iron. In spite of the problems, her balance and straightness were remarkably good. Even if the horse unexpectedly quickened the pace or shied, she still coped, although her reactions were slightly delayed.

To help keep the left foot in the stirrup, she had placed a strip of elastic (John Smart's suggestion) over the stirrup iron and foot. To help the left arm, I experimented with a little leather strap on the front of my own saddle. This I showed to Georgina and asked her if she would like to try it. She liked the idea and the saddler made one for her.

The months flashed by and she was now jumping also. She reached her first goal of qualifying for the Championships. She did well there until she was forced to withdraw after the cross-country, as the horse injured himself. This put an end to training with Folly.

We had our laughs, but never tears.

By the following year, 1979, she had acquired a new horse and competition was again the theme, coupled with taking her Pony Club 'A' test. Her left side had made some improvement throughout the winter, but there was still a long way to go. The arm was still jerky and the left leg was still inclined to contract. Georgina, with her great determination, was ready to work hard again and at times it took great tact to go slow enough. I had to remind her that Rome wasn't built in a day!

With the 'A' test in sight, I knew there was still quite a lot to achieve. My next step was to lunge her to improve coordination. This is a wonderful and invaluable exercise for all riders, and Georgina found it extremely beneficial as it gave her the opportunity to concentrate exclusively on herself and not on the horse.

For the exam, riding is not all that is required. Theory also plays an important role. This at first was a big struggle for Georgina. She would always start the answer but often had difficulty in expressing herself or finding the right words. If she drew a blank, she would say, 'You know what I mean.' In fact, I did know what she was trying to say, so I would either give her a new lead or suggest a word. This built up her confidence and answering questions definitely became a lot easier.

I also gave her the theoretical discussion away from her horse around the stable-yard. These discussions were the big 'hump'. Her powers of concentration were lost and she easily became tired and therefore more muddled. However, we persevered. She wrote notes and I set her questions to write in her own time and corrected them on the next visit.

For the 'A' test, one is required to ride different horses, so I decided to give Georgina the experience of riding my horses. I might add that they were high-powered competition horses, but because of her natural talent, she was relaxed and seldom interfered with them, so they liked her and went kindly for her.

We would meet up at events and I would advise her and walk the cross-country courses with her. Her gait was still unbalanced – the left side still not functioning normally, causing her to take a shorter step. This of course made her slower and her agility to climb round fences or tricky terrain was hindered. I did in fact myself walk a little slower, but if she got left behind, I would spend extra time studying a fence. I would give her a helping hand when necessary and would at times get her to assist me, while crossing a ditch for example. I never wanted her to feel that she was hindering me or that I was treating her differently from any other competitor.

She competed with success in the BHS (British Horse Society) events – a remarkable achievement.

That autumn, I suggested that she visit an osteopath, but of course that she should discuss it with her doctors and family first. She went for treatment, which in particular helped the muscles in her left arm and elbow.

We continued with the lessons and met at events. She attempted the 'A' test but without success.

Exam tension proved to be the problem and coming up against strangers brought back the speech difficulties. However, Georgina was not to be beaten. She was also keen to develop her skills as an instructor, to test herself even more. We worked at this as well. She finally passed her 'A' test in 1982.

In that year competition resulted in success. Again Georgina, not being satisfied to stand still, commenced training for the next instructor's exam. I told her this would be some way off as theory played a very large part and therefore demanded many hours of concentration. She sneakily put herself into the exam and telephoned me with a failure. She accepted the ups and downs and could always face me when it came to the crunch. My advice was now to 'cool it', go on gaining experience and confidence and retake the exam at a later date.

For the end of that year, Georgina invited me on a trip to Kenya. A week's safari and a week on the coast were a perfect combination.

During the next few years Georgina continued with her tuition and studies and in 1985 she added yet another exam to her credit by qualifying as a Dressage judge, upgrading to List 4 in 1987.

Georgina is now looking after and competing with two, if not three horses, so her daily schedule is somewhat full. Distance and time prevent regular visits for tuition, but as soon as the chips are down or she has a problem, she is on the phone and comes over at the earliest opportunity for a sort out.

I still admire her courage and determination. Her

fight back into top-level competition in a sport which almost killed her is a fine example to many.

The initial bond has remained between us and indeed we are great friends. During our holiday in Kenya, over seven years ago, we were lying one day by the pool in the heat of the sun when Georgina came up with the idea of writing a book. We discussed this at length and we even got as far as deciding on chapter headings. I knew that she was serious about this idea and I felt sure that in time I would see her book on the shelf.

The Pony Club tests, formulated under the auspices of the British Horse Society, start at 'D', where the eight- or nine-year-old has to show confidence in handling and riding a pony, with a little basic horsemanship thrown in. Later the 'C' test requires the eleven- or twelve-year-olds to ride safely on roads and in the countryside, at all paces and over small jumps. There is also a stable-management test, involving such subjects as feeding, tack, shoeing, and veterinary matters. There is then a 'C plus' test that bridges the gap between 'C' and 'B'. The 'B' test is taken from the age of fourteen and involves riding other candidates' mounts as well as one's own. The next step is the 'H' test, on stable management, usually taken when the child is on the threshold of young adulthood and has developed his own ideas.

I had taken my 'D' and 'C' tests on the same day in September 1969 when I was eight years old, and my 'C plus' when I was ten. I took the 'B' test in 1975 and was working towards the 'H' test before I had my accident. I was determined not to miss out. Our local test was scheduled by chance for Remembrance Sunday in 1978, about seventeen months after my fall, and although I was confident that I knew my subject, I was worried about my ability to answer questions because I was still having difficulties in concentrating. Particularly difficult was lecturing on a given subject for a specified time. Somehow I came through.

The 'A' test is the supreme Pony Club exam. It involves riding a number of animals unknown to you and assessing them and their problems, and giving advice on how to improve them. The second part deals with theory, right across the spectrum from handling horses to stable construction, clothing the horse, grooming, the care and fitting of tack, clipping and trimming, feeding, forage, bedding, shoeing, and health, condition, excercise and fitness, first aid, horse conformation, and so on. Candidates who pass the first two parts then go on to advanced riding on trained horses, performing specialist movements, usually indoors.

When I took my 'A' test in 1981, although four years had elapsed since the accident, I was still not my normal self. There were still problems with balance and I still found it difficult to do full justice to myself when it came to answering questions. I was therefore probably tenser than I should have been. All candidates are nervous of such an examination but perhaps I had more cause to be.

It should not have come as a surprise that I failed my first 'A' test, but I had never failed any test before, and I felt very demoralised, especially as everything seemed to have gone well and I got into the third and final phase. All the horses settled for me and I believed that I had answered the theoretical questions correctly and without jumbling my words.

I put my failure down to my left arm. It was no longer flapping but it remained stiff and unattractive from the shoulder down to the elbow, and this must have affected the examiners, if not the horses. The head examiner told me that, in my condition, I was no more likely to pass the test than she was to become Prime Minister! I was completely demolished by this comment, when a glimmer of hope would have given me some encouragement.

For the record, I tried again the following year. I felt more secure this time, both physically and mentally, especially having just passed my driving test. Driving had been far more difficult than riding, which was more natural to me. Again coordination had been the problem, but now I had qualified and was able to drive myself to Benenden for the 'A' test. This time I was the only candidate to survive the first two phases, and this time I passed. I was of course elated. I felt like telephoning last year's examiner and advising her to apply for Mrs Thatcher's job.

Through all this time, I was receiving help from many different people, not forgetting my self-sacrificing parents and family. I went occasionally to see Addie Raeburn at the Tower of London. She used to have me lying on an enormous sofa while she held my head and somehow I always drifted into sleep, during which, she tells me, she held my elbow. When I awoke, it was much more flexible and after, I think, my third visit I was able to straighten my arm without discomfort.

Tessa continued her good work and constantly helped

me to improve, not only with my riding but in many other ways also. Her time, of course, with me was limited, and she also travelled a lot, examining and teaching, both in this country and overseas. My other riding teacher, John Smart, went to the Isle of Man, so I enlisted the aid of Colin Wares to help me with my jumping. Colin, well known as an international horse-trials and show-jumping rider, had taken part in no fewer than eight Badmintons, so it was a privilege to be taught by him. He never allowed my physical stiffness, or anything else, to affect his programmes for me. He told me one day, after a cross-country practice, that, as I was approaching the more difficult fences, he had suddenly seen a light come on in my face, and after a rather messy start I had jumped like a real rider. I was riding Tullig that day, which is Irish for 'Rock', betraying his origins. He was bred by Eric Horgan, who rode Pontoon for Ireland in the 1976 Olympics. My parents had bought Tullig for me in 1978 after Folly developed leg problems. He was the biggest horse I have ever ridden – a bay gelding, 16.3 hands high.

The following year we found another Irish gelding who looked as though he might make the grade. This was Smurf, as he was known in the stables, although his competition name was Jaunty Jaeger. Smurf was important because he introduced me to Teresa Elwell, or to be more correct it was Colin who made the introduction when he advised me to consult Teresa about Smurf's back. There was a problem with his jumping style and we thought that an experienced chiropractor would be worth a try.

On the principle that what is good enough for a horse must be good enough for a human, after seeing how well Teresa's treatment worked on Smurf, I asked her to have a go at me. She discovered things that I did not know were wrong. Addie Raeburn had always reckoned that my neck was damaged but now Teresa confirmed that not only was a vertebra in my neck misaligned but that I also had a tilted pelvis.

After manipulation by Teresa, I felt wonderfully different. I had not until then realised what pain I had been suffering. It was only when it was removed that I understood what I had had to put up with. Only those who have been in pain can appreciate the feeling of relief when it disappears. Teresa warned me that it would take time for the muscles and ligaments to rearrange themselves, but I really began to believe from that time onwards that recovery was on its way.

Teresa Elwell (chiropractor)

I think it might help to define what I do before we discuss Georgina Colthurst – or rather the horses first, because our association started with them.

I practise chiropractic, a method of healing where the spinal column is adjusted physically to remove or obviate nerve interference.

I was originally taught to apply this method to humans, as was my brother, the trainer Anthony Webber; and then, after tuition by the great Ronnie Longford, we went on to treat horses, and eventually other animals too.

I first treated Jaunty Jaeger at the Frensham stables for a back problem and we agreed that I should visit the Colthurst home in Kent for follow-up therapy for Smurf, as he was known. He did not pose any serious problems. I wish all cases were as straightforward as his, and they would be if only one could get to the problem immediately. It is when the back has been distorted for any length of time that we have difficulty. Then, the muscle will have adapted to the distortion and however much you set the spine straight, those warped muscles will tend to pull it back to misalignment. So that means special exercises to make the muscles do their proper job, which complicates and lengthens the healing process.

But either way, it works. We reckon to put back into their original roles at least 95 per cent of all our animals, and that includes everything from show ponies to one-ton dray heavies, and from riding-school hacks to international jumpers, not forgetting eventers and racehorses – and sometimes also their riders.

It was after we came in from Smurf's box, over coffee in the Colthurst sitting room, when we were chatting about her 1977 experiences, that Georgina wondered if I could help with her own problems – specifically, a sore neck and painful lower back.

I was not too sure about that, because aside from that horrendous incident, she had had heavy falls before and since – every serious horseman comes off from time to time – and in fact she admitted that she had just had quite a tumble. This can lead to long-established conditions, some of which may be untreatable. However, I had a look.

Every back tells a story. With Georgina's, her Atlas vertebra – the first one, up in the neck – was out of line, with the muscle around it wasted as a result, and as her pelvis was also clearly tipped and crooked, it was small wonder that she was in pain. Her condition was distorting the skeins of nerves passing down inside her spine.

After a little remedial pressure on the correct transverse processes, and a suitable rotation of her pelvis, I had her smiling in astonishment as she sat up.

Chiropractic is not a one-off, heal-and-go matter. Often, and most usually with chronic or historical problems like Georgina's, the treatment has to be repeated, perhaps over months or even years. Our difficulty was simply geography: from their Crockham Hill to our Cropredy it is almost a hundred miles as the crow flies. Nevertheless we did manage to coincide five or six times a year, and in the more recent eventing seasons my brother Anthony has weighed in too, and not always using nice civilised treatment rooms – they often had to meet up where his travels crossed with Georgina's eventing excursions. Typically, this happened sometimes in lay-bys – a favourite was the M25's Exit 8 slip road, where once he straightened her up in a blizzard.

I do not set out to sell this alternative medicine for my own ends. I have more than enough patients, both animal and human, to keep me happy. But it is heartening to see that in the last twenty years or so, conventional medicine has more and more acknowledged that people like Anthony and I can and do achieve results where other therapies have failed. In many ways, and especially in helping those as courageous and determined as Georgina Colthurst, that is reward enough.

In 1982, at Tessa's suggestion in preparation for my 'A' test, I first started going to a specialist dressage trainer named Pat Manning, who has a yard near Reading, and is one of the finest teachers of instruction in the country. She is wonderfully perceptive and kind and seldom raises her voice, and she encourages you to give your best.

She helped me, among other things, to project my voice and thereby become more confident in teaching others. This was particularly important when I became a dressage judge in July 1983 and when I took the BHS Intermediate Instructors test in October 1983. I am sure that my success in passing this test had a lot to do with both Tessa and Pat, who helped to make my year full of steady and rewarding progress, with only one disaster.

Falls are a natural hazard for any rider and are accepted as part of the job. They are never pleasant but perhaps on occasion they are good for the soul. There is no better leveller than a horse. Just after I had become a dressage judge, I took part in a competition with a young and inexperienced horse who, perhaps blinded by the sun, failed to take off at a solid white fence, which he almost uprooted. He broke his knee and rolled over me.

My main concern was for the horse and it was not at first

apparent to me how serious his injury was. Although lame, he was able to walk back to the lorry in which we drove him home. It was only later, following an X-ray, that the extent of the damage became clear.

I myself felt very sore and in need of Teresa's magic hands. By coincidence I was supposed to go to a party she was giving that night but I was too crippled to travel. I found it difficult to breathe and impossible to find a comfortable position in which to sit or lie. This was my first bad fall since the disaster of 1977. My parents, who must have been worried, remained seemingly calm, but in fact I had dislodged my pelvis and cracked a bone in my neck and two ribs.

I tried not to let this fall interrupt my life. In fact I took part in a competition the following week, despite my parents' doubts, and was placed quite high.

I had another fall the following year, at Windsor Forest Novice Horse Trials. This time a young horse was over-bold, and I found myself back at St Thomas's – but only overnight while they stitched a bad cut above my right eye. It was a strange and nasty experience for me to be back in a place that held so many miserable memories. In the morning, before I was released, one of the doctors asked whether I had ever thought of giving up riding. Did I not regard it as a dangerous sport? I replied that one could have an accident driving a car.

I had to stop riding for three weeks because I could not put any sort of riding hat on my head and Sarah Whitmore, who lives nearby, came to the rescue by exercising our horses. I again needed Teresa to straighten me out, and she, along with Tessa, Pat Manning and Colin Wares saw me through all my ups and downs.

Fortunately from there onwards, there were more ups than downs. In October 1986, I was chosen with my horse, Wily Woodpecker, whom we knew as Woody, to represent Britain at the International Three-Day Event in Boekolo in Holland.

Woody had come to us as a six-year-old through Colin Wares in 1983, when Smurf had left us and Tullig had become injured. It was a tragedy when Tullig broke his splint bones, because he had enormous scope. Woody had been very successful in the show ring but had never horse-trialled. He was not easy at dressage early on but was a natural jumper. He had a habit of spooking or shying away from birds or things he thought strange, which is another way of saying that he had a very active brain. He was the first horse I upgraded to Advanced status. His consistent form led to his selection for the British squad.

The actual British team of four, which won the event, consisted of Lucinda Green, Lorna Clarke, Karen Straker and Rodney Powell. This left me and the other members of the squad to ride as individuals. I was really pleased to have this opportunity. Woody travelled very well and seemed to enjoy his new surroundings and the atmosphere. He was third overall of the British entries in the dressage and he went well cross-country until he spotted two donkeys. They were attached to either end of a plank and their function was to walk round to generate water under a particular fence. As we approached, he spooked at the donkeys instead of concentrating on the fence, and stopped. We got over at the second attempt but, having decided not to push him to enable him to concentrate on the remaining jumps, which he cleared easily, we had some time faults. He was one of only three British horses to do a clear round in the show-jumping.

This was a fantastic experience for me, and probably for Woody too. Sadly he hurt his pelvis the following year and has since left us to go hunting.

I felt that by this time, nine years after the accident, I was pretty well recovered. The occasional fall had nothing to do with my condition but with my activity. I suppose that in one or two small respects I was slightly imperfect. The left side of my body – more particularly my arm and shoulder – was no longer obviously stiff and awkward, but I knew that it was less good than my right. I also knew that it lacked the elasticity of my right side. One further problem was that I became over-tired too easily.

It was at the suggestion of Addie Raeburn that I first consulted a cranial osteopath in 1986, who indicated that I may not have been as cured as I believed.

Solihin Thom (cranial osteopath)

Cranium being understood as the bone structure of the head, and osteopathy as treatment by manipulation, many people think my calling a confusion of terms. There is often the puzzled question: 'How on earth can the skull be manipulated? Isn't it bone?'

The answer lies in proper definition. For more accurately, the cranium is the group of bones which enclose the brain. These, we are able to influence and so help the brain function better.

140

It was Adeline Raeburn with her open approach to healing, and knowing of my success with head-injured people, who referred Georgina Colthurst to me.

I was much impressed by the young woman from the moment when she stepped into my Fulham surgery almost nine years after her accident. Her problems were some confusion and social gaucherie, together with general lack of coordination. After hearing about the initiating fall and its aftermath, and then of those before and since, I was pretty confident that her essential brain mobility had been impaired.

The brain should expand and contract about a dozen times a minute in very fine but definite movements, each vital for an efficient and healthy organ. I felt that was not happening here, and with her skull in my hands, so it proved. Her cranian membranes were rigid and flat. The structural integrity of the brain inside could not operate as it should, that is, back to front, top to bottom, side to side, in a rhythmic cycle once each six seconds or so.

Through palpation – the sensing with one's hands – we were able to define the extent of the problems. From there, and from then in much the same manner as the body osteopath, I could act: that is, I set up gentle 'moulding' pressures to encourage release and movement, and normal patterns in their regular cadences, in each part of her head.

Cranial osteopathy is not yet accepted by conventional medicine, but there certainly is overwhelming proof of success, and thousands of practitioners of conventional medicine, from GPs to consultants, refer patients to such as myself for a broad spectrum of complaints.

As one appointment succeeded another, the anomalies of Georgina's original presentation began to right themselves, to her undisguised relief and happiness. Through improved brain functioning, the disorganised behaviour started receding and, as it were, she began to come together. Her facial movement, control and therefore expressions came first: quite early on she began to use the left side better – mouth and lip control made her speech clearer, and she started to smile, using the whole of her face as the partial paralysis disappeared.

At the same time her walking improved. The left foot, from sometimes slapping down awkwardly, now always struck the floor decisively as her subconscious recalled what she had first learned as an infant, which had been wiped out by her injury, and which had been only partly re-assimilated by her prodigious will-power and conscious effort, before we came together.

All this one watched with extreme care. We were not after results from that applied will-power: what we wanted was the brain itself recalling skills from her subconscious, in instinctive use – in short, getting back to true normality.

One could go further into the why's and wherefore's of cranial osteopathy, but this is one person's story over one period of time, and not a medical tract. The tale is basically of underlying faith, and of that more than in almost any other of my patients. Her recovery in my hands from the first has been a matter of: 'Come on, get it together, I'm going to get better,' and with a determination bordering on impatience that I found not always easy to contain or deflect in her best interests.

When the patient's brain says that, it is probably the normality that we have, together, done all we can to achieve.

Since my accident, which of course was totally unexpected, my mind has been opened to similar problems experienced by other people. My own grandfather, for example, was nearly killed in a car crash when I was a child. He was paralysed and unable to speak, and the frustration for such an active man is something that I can now really appreciate. Later he had a heart attack and, having suffered a sudden disaster myself, I am now aware of the similarities between different classes of physical disaster. I hope in fact that my book will encourage and help not only those who have sustained head injuries, for instance, but will be of benefit to anyone in any way disabled.

I have also discovered – and I want to make this point very clearly – that the medical profession is understandably cautious when dealing with patients, often too cautious to the point of being pessimistic, and communicating that pessimism to the patients' families and friends. How can an invalid be hopeful about his condition if all around him are spreading gloom? Hope is the first step on the ladder to cure. One must be motivated to get well and have an incentive, but how is this possible if everybody accepts the worst?

I am not complaining about the wonderful doctors who looked after me but there was one who told my parents that I would never fully recover and that my left arm would never straighten. He said it would be ten years before I would be able to go to a party on my own. (I actually proved him wrong by nine and three-quarter years!) He told a friend, Diana Wilson, that I would never ride again. Thank God she did not pass on this misinformation to me or my parents, although I would never have accepted it anyway. In these situations, one must never despair but I must admit that there were times when I felt that life was not worth carrying on. I blew hot and cold mentally, sometimes almost abandoning hope but at other times strong in my determination to recover. A sense of humour, even in the most adverse circumstances, is a wonderful asset. You must try to laugh at yourself if possible. I have been helped enormously by 'alternative medicine', as it is nowadays called, and perhaps one of the best therapies is humour.

Rehabilitation was a long process, although I resumed activity far sooner than most people had expected. Over twelve years later, I regard myself as 98 per cent better and I lead a completely normal life.

I am aware that some people think I am mad but at least I am pursuing the sport I love when many people reckoned I would still be a cabbage. Of course it is a demanding sport that requires full fitness and I have always been a fitness fanatic, but sometimes a good mental attitude can be in part a substitute for physical condition.

I still feel that I missed a good two years out of my life, although I was very active during that time. I lacked the confidence to mix easily with people and I was uncomfortable about going anywhere on my own. I had trouble passing my driving test and when I succeeded, this gave me a great boost. At last I felt independent again.

I had to sit a number of riding exams and I was aware that the examiners may have been nervous about passing me. They seemed always to be looking for faults, but I managed to get over this problem.

When I read Bob Champion's autobiography, I was reminded how similar his experiences were to mine, although in a different way and for different reasons. Like him, I want to show that the impossible is sometimes possible.

Lady Colthurst

When Georgina was still in the Brook unconscious, and we were spending as much time as possible with her, the nurses in the ward said we should be saving our energy as we would need it all if and when she came home. At the time we did not realise how true this was.

We first brought her home from St Thomas's for a weekend, as we thought that home surroundings would settle her down. The drive home by car was traumatic as Georgina very quickly became exhausted and could not wait to get home. Having eventually arrived back, she went straight to bed and to sleep, and over the weekend we gave her none of the sleeping pills she had had in hospital. We felt that after seven weeks it was time for her to wake up. She could not talk, walk, feed or dress herself, so the weekend was busy, but she became so much happier in herself that we decided we would try and keep her at home and hope that, between us all, we could manage.

The days were exhaustingly full, looking after her in every way, but we were lucky that it was holiday time and one or other of the boys was always at home to help me. She could not be left alone in the house at any time for the first few months and I was fortunate to have someone who could come in while I went shopping. You have to be prepared to make rehabilitation a full-time job if it has any chance of being a success, and this becomes quite a strain on the family as many things have to be given up or put to one side. We felt it a duty to help Georgina in every way, and the pleasure it gave us when improvements were made was well worthwhile. Having to take her everywhere was time-consuming.

Many head-injured patients seem to go through childhood again before recovering properly, and we gradually learnt that things we thought unusual are very common. Georgina had an almost insatiable thirst for everything, and having lost a terrific amount of weight, soon became too fat. This in turn was a problem as clothes and above all riding boots would no longer fit, causing misery. We had to regulate food and drink.

Memory – both long- and short-term – was lacking and we asked endless questions to try and get it working again, starting with what happened only a few months ago. This was boring but the repetition worked. She also had no idea of the time of day – morning or evening.

Luckily Georgina was anxious to improve, but many times she was exceedingly depressed as everything was so slow, or did not work properly. The best encouragement on black days was to point out that one week things had been done which were impossible the previous week.

Depression was always a problem, particularly early on, as also was frustration when she could no longer do things which had been easy before. Occasional rages were brought on by this.

Her speech was badly slurred at first, and a monotone. Gradually normal intonation returned and the slurred voice only recurred when she was tired.

It is essential for the patient to have an interest and aim. With Georgina it was horses. As Mr Neil-Dwyer, the neurosurgeon, told us, this provides the stimulation essential to recovery. Without something to strive for, there is little point in the endless slog to get better. He considered the risk in riding was less important than the benefits to be gained. Many people were critical of this, without knowing either the facts or the professional advice given.

Complete lack of concentration was another

problem. Asking Georgina questions about simple things she had read or seen seemed to help. Coordination gradually improved, and we assisted this by easy exercises, playing card games and Scrabble.

Patients try to prove themselves and show they can do things themselves – not always appreciated by the families who fear disaster. They have to be allowed to do as much as possible because this boosts their morale. Georgina was determined throughout and this helped her to recover. She had a longing to be independent but often lacked confidence to do things on her own. She needed much encouragement and prodding from the family even to do simple things like buying a newspaper or toothpaste.

Probably the most essential ingredient to recovery is rest. Patients get exhausted extremely quickly, and sleep is a great healer.

Since Georgina's accident, the National Head Injuries Association has started an organisation called Headway to help the victims of head injuries and their relations. The organisation's aims are to raise public awareness of the head-injured and their difficulties; and to encourage research and campaign for further rehabilitation and residential facilities for head-injured people. Local support groups give advice and counselling to head-injured persons and to their relatives and friends and help with the resettlement of the injured people at home, dealing with problems of concentration, memory and behaviour. There are now over eighty branches in the British Isles, and in most places meetings take place at least monthly. These are an enormous help as friends and relations can discuss problems, find out what is unusual or not, and above all have a chat and gain much encouragement. It can be lonely looking after an injured person, and always tiring, and it is most reassuring to find that others have similar problems.

In general the medical profession seems to give unnervingly pessimistic views of head injuries which, although understandable, can be exceedingly depressing for relations, and in fact are often proved wrong. We were told by an eminent retired neurosurgeon that even today the brain is still something of an unknown quantity and no one can give an accurate prediction of recovery. Without hope, there is little point in all the hard work involved, and most Headway families have proved that with time, determination and encouragement, many patients improve way beyond the original medical prognosis. Headway have also started day centres for the head-injured, giving the latter a day out with companions and occupational therapy, and the relations a much needed break.

Sir Richard Colthurst, Bart (father)

My father had always said, 'While there's life, there's hope.' After the dreadful shock of being told that Georgina's chances of survival were only fifty-fifty, we pinned everything on not accepting defeat but constantly seeking a positive, successful outcome. It was explained to us, however, that head injuries can take years to heal.

When confronted by a situation like this, one finds oneself in an unreal world. Time seems to stand still and nothing appears to happen. It is almost like being in a dream. I remember a house surgeon asking me what my job was. It seemed a peculiarly irrelevant question at the time and I replied: 'My job is to get my daughter better.' A similar reply was given by a docker whose son, in the next bed to Georgina, had suffered head injuries as a result of being run over by a car.

My wife and I learnt a great deal about recovery during our experience with Georgina, especially by rubbing shoulders with the families of other injured people. We were lucky to have a large enough family ourselves to spread the load of being in constant attendance. I used to read extracts to Georgina while she was in hospital from *The Ponies of Bunts* and other books which we knew she had once liked, in the hope of engaging her attention.

We took advice from everybody, including the hospital tea-lady, who told us that the doctors and nurses thought they had all the answers but that really we should also adopt the approach of the *Scientific Review*. She thrust into my hand a copy of this journal, which encourages people to hold prayer groups to carry out the Biblical instruction that 'When two or three are gathered together in Thy name, Thou wilt grant their requests'. As it happened, we already had three of these groups going! We would have tried anything or anybody to help our daughter – even a witchdoctor, had one been on hand.

Mr Northcroft, the previous boss of the head unit at the Brook, gave us hope when he sensibly pointed out that head-injured victims of accidents either survived or died; if they survived, they either recovered fully or they had a problem; if they had a problem, then they would have to be helped. I asked how we were placed.

'You seem to be living,' he said.

'Good,' I said, 'so what now?'

'We cannot tell yet,' he replied.

He did, however, give us examples of remarkable recoveries, and this encouraged us greatly at the time. When eventually Georgina came out of her coma, we set about helping her to full recovery.

In 1982 she was competing in the Windsor Three-Day Event horse trials where Riding for the Disabled were holding a meeting. She was invited to sit on the stage with three or four others to answer questions. After a while, the Chairman told the meeting that Georgina had to leave to ride her horse over the cross-country phase. There was a hush, then great applause, as many in the audience realised that she was sufficiently recovered to take part. This seemed to give them all immense pleasure. They must have felt that there was hope for them too.

The days of recovery had seemed endless, yet in the end it all came right, thus proving another old saying: 'Time is a great healer.'

If what Georgina has managed to accomplish truly shows what can be done when all seems lost, then every minute taken by each one of us could not have been better spent.

Nigel Taylor – 1990 (international event rider)

Being very deeply involved in the eventing world, I was well aware of Georgina's problems relating to her riding accident and her very determined efforts to re-establish herself as a leading event rider.

I first met Georgina as a fellow competitor in the 1989 eventing season and we first worked together when she applied to attend a dressage clinic held by Christopher Bartle at my base, the Milton Keynes Eventing Centre, in February 1990. She came to the clinic, performed well and thoroughly enjoyed it. During the clinic she asked me to school her over some cross-country fences on her present horses, Limerick Lear and Blarney Bonus. As we have a wide range of fences from pre-novice to advanced standard, I thought I would try her on some of the 'easy' ones. This was definitely *not* what Georgina had in mind. She wanted to practise over our advanced and therefore most difficult fences.

She performed well at all types of fence but was

very insistent on practising at the water complex.
There are several alternatives at this jump and
Georgina wanted to try the most difficult approach.
Her first two attempts resulted in her getting very
wet (it is fortunate that she is a strong swimmer!),
but falls are considered part and parcel of our sport.
She and Blarney Bonus were not too sure about the
water to start with, but after several attempts they
became confident, and, despite being soaked
through, Georgina kept going until she was 'water
perfect'.

Since then she has been back several times for
more schooling and she and her horses have
improved on every visit. We have also been
competing against each other at some of the early
events this year and I am pleased at the way my
'pupil' is performing.

The dedication that Georgina shows for the love of
horses and riding, and the tenacity in her character,
are quite extraordinary and undoubtedly helped her
to make such a recovery from her accident. I hope
that this will be rewarded in competitions, as she
looks and acts like a rider who wants to reach the top
in her chosen sport. I hope that I can continue to help
her realise her ambition to become one of our leading
international event riders.

Looking back now, over twelve years after my accident, I
can picture myself regaining semi-consciousness in a
strange hospital, uncertain where I was or why I was there,

uncertain even who I was, and almost totally unable to move or communicate in any way.

I was terrified, wondering whether I was myself or somebody else, wondering whether I was alive or dead, whether I was in the real world or in a nightmare. I felt instinctively that I was in some sort of prison from which I had to escape.

I know that I would not be here today, leading an active existence, but for two things: a determination to return to normality against all odds, and wonderful support and care from family, friends and therapists (including the horses!).

I experienced tremendous frustration, appalling depression and any number of setbacks, but I have also learnt the value of fitness and that one must never despair. A positive attitude definitely encourages improvement. This goes of course for head-injured patients but it surely applies to everyone who is disabled.

It is wonderful for me that I can now face the future, and I hope that my experience may help others to look forward to better things.

As regards my future, I am now very hopeful and even ambitious. I find training and bringing young horses up to a high standard very rewarding, and I would like to compete in more major competitions and upgrade as a dressage judge.

In addition to teaching horses, I enjoy helping humans, and since my injury many people have come to me for advice, or written to me, who have had head injuries and want to become mobile again or who have had to look after disabled people. It may be that one day I will take up physiotherapy, or some such activity, because I have been told that I appear to have developed some sort of natural healing process through my hands – perhaps as a result of my injury, who knows?

At least I have that possibility when only a few years ago a number of people gave me up for dead.